MW01123765

NORICK

The Mayors of Oklahoma City

BY BILL MOORE
AND RICK MOORE

SERIES EDITOR: GINI MOORE CAMPBELL
ASSOCIATE EDITOR: ERIC DABNEY

OKLAHOMA
HERITAGE
ASSOCIATION

Oklahoma City

ISBN 1-885596-50-2
Library of Congress Catalog Number 2005938024
Book cover and contents designed by Sandi Welch/www.2WDesignGroup.com

CONTENTS

Acknowledgments   5
Foreword by Governor George Nigh   11
Foreword by Governor Frank Keating   12

CHAPTER I: Norick History   19
CHAPTER II: The First Election   39
CHAPTER III: City Councilman Jim Norick   49
CHAPTER IV: The First Run for Mayor   59
CHAPTER V: Mayor Jim   69
CHAPTER VI: Water for Oklahoma City   81
CHAPTER VII: Re-election   93
CHAPTER VIII: Second Chance   101
CHAPTER IX: The Garbage Strike   121
CHAPTER X: The Next Generation   135
CHAPTER XI: The Character of Ron Norick   143
CHAPTER XII: Ron Norick the Politician   161
CHAPTER XIII: Ron's First Term   173
CHAPTER XIV: The Birth of MAPS: The Rebirth of a City   189
CHAPTER XV: April 19, 1995: The Day that Shocked a Country   221
CHAPTER XVI: The Last Term   239

Epilogue   259
APPENDIX A: *Mayors of Oklahoma City*   275
APPENDIX B: *James Norick Time Line*   277
APPENDIX C: *Ronald Norick Time Line*   291
APPENDIX D: *Norick Documents*   297
Bibliography   305
Endnotes   307
Index   315

ACKNOWLEDGMENTS

BILL MOORE

THIS HISTORIC PRESENTATION OF THE LIVES of two legends in Oklahoma City government did not happen overnight. Jim and Ron Norick are not the type to brag about themselves. They are more likely to tell what others have done or how each tried to do his best. Fortunately, their wonderful story can be told through the historic records and the testimonies of the many individuals who came in contact with them through the years.

We had no problem getting interviews with people in this community. Everyone wanted to join in and tell how much these two men have meant to Oklahoma City. We are indebted to all of the kind folks who returned our calls and gave of their time for interviews.

My brother and I were born in this city and have been alive during the Norick administrations. We are better people because of their contributions to our community and feel it a privilege to tell their story.

I have had some great help as I've gone about my work on this book. Chad Williams, Manuscript Archivist at Oklahoma

Historical Society was exceptionally helpful in getting access to the James Norick Collection. Lillie Kerr helped with photos in the OHS Photo Archives.

Newspaper stories provide a solid basis for most research. With that said, I would like to thank Steve Lackmeyer, Jack Money, and all of the reporters whose stories through the years have provided the day-by-day record of events. I also want to give a special thanks to Mary Phillips, News Research Specialist at *The Daily Oklahoman*, for her great help with some special photos.

Carleen Holman and Kaye Olsmith at Norick Investments have been a tremendous help throughout this process in getting information to and from Jim and Ron. These two ladies were always pleasant and helped in any way they could.

Governors Nigh and Keating have been wonderful to work with and their forewords tell a part of this great story. Their leadership at the state level is legend itself.

Gini Campbell at the Oklahoma Heritage Association is always a pleasure to work with. Her smile and professional help with the project goes above and beyond. Bob Burke is always there to help and I certainly appreciate his encouragement and support.

It has been a true honor to tell the stories of two of Oklahoma City's finest mayors. Both men are what American politics should be about: unpretentious individuals, visionaries, and great leaders. Of all the things I accomplish in life, this chronicle of their lives will always be a high point.

Finally, it is an amazing thing to have written a book with my brother. Our family has always discussed current affairs over dinner and to share this with my brother is a great experience. His work in politics and my work in history made a natural combination to produce this book. I hope it serves well to tell this story of the last half of the first century of Oklahoma City's life and the two men who led us through it.

THIS IS MY FIRST BOOK PROJECT, and it was a humbling experience for me to say the least. Luckily, the story we were writing about was one that was a pleasure to do. Jim and Ron Norick have left their fingerprints and footsteps all over the City of Oklahoma City. They did more to make this City a better place to live and raise a family during their 5 terms in office, than probably the rest of the mayors in our history combined. That is not a negative on any of our other mayors, but rather a huge positive about these two men. It was truly a privilege to try and record their efforts. Their story truly deserves to be told and retold for years to come.

It was also a special joy and privilege for me to get to work with my brother on this project. He was truly a guiding light for me in this project, and I could never have done this book without his efforts. His journalism training and historical knowledge kept me going down the right path. Thanks, Bill.

This seemed like it took forever to complete, but an event took place during this project that ripped my heart right out of my chest, and made it hard to go on. Our dad died in early 2002, and his sudden loss was devastating to us both. Dad was our best friend, and mentor. But we realized that he would want us to go on and complete this book, so he became our inspiration. It is to his memory that we dedicate this book.

This book also took a lot of help from a lot of other people. Carleen Holman and Kaye Olsmith, who work at Norick Investments, were great helps throughout the years we worked on this book, and we owe them a debt of gratitude. Laure Vaught Majors of FSB was a great help in locating graphics of the original MAPS drawings.

From the City of Oklahoma City, there was the ever-present Executive Secretary to the Mayor, Fran Cory. Fran was a blessing to have because of her years of knowledge at City Hall to help us find things for the book. My good friend Craig Keith, Assistant Municipal Counselor at the City was a tremendous resource for documents and statistics. Linda Bull, Secretary to the Trust at the McGee Creek Authority and an Office Specialist in the Water Department went above and beyond the call of duty in helping us locate pictures. Mario Quiroga in the Public Information and Marketing Office was invaluable in helping us get some pictures and other documents. I would also like to thank my friend, Jim Thompson, Assistant City Manager of the City of Oklahoma City, for his willingness to help in the research of this book.

Thanks to Gini Campbell at the Oklahoma Heritage Association for being the professional she is and keeping me going in the right direction. Her leadership was important to the project. Thanks to the most prolific author I have ever had the pleasure to know, Bob Burke. He was incredibly helpful in acquiring historical pictures, and being a real inspiration to me throughout this process.

Thanks to all those who we interviewed to get the stories we tell in these pages. Rick Horrow, of Horrow Sports Ventures in Miami, Florida is a great friend, and his book When The Game Is On The Line, was a great resource for some of the events during MAPS. City Councilman Gary Marrs, former City Manager Don Bown, Lt. Governor Mary Fallin, former Governor Frank Keating, Jim Bruza of FSB architects to name just a few, were all eager participants and extremely open about their dealings with Ron Norick, and for that I am eternally grateful.

A special thank you goes out to former Governors George Nigh and Frank Keating for their incredibly warm and touching foreword to this book. Their friendship has always meant a lot to me, and their willingness to participate in this project was nothing short of wonderful.

Working for Ron Norick in my position as Assistant to the Mayor for over eight years was the happiest time in my public career. Every evening when I came home from work, I felt like we had accomplished something good that day to make Oklahoma City a better place to live and work. The reason this happened was Ron Norick and this book is a small way for me to thank him for that experience.

And finally, I want to thank my wife, Vickie and our kids who had to put up with my late-night work on the computer, the stacks of pictures and papers and documents in my home office, and constantly being a sounding board to my writings. I truly could not have survived this project without your care, love and support. Thank you from the bottom of my heart.

FOREWORD

BY GOVERNOR GEORGE NIGH

To be perfectly honest, I haven't the slightest idea when I met Jim Norick. It was just one of those things that happened along the way. Whenever it was, wherever it was, it was the beginning of one of the best friendships that a guy could have. A bonus was the first hand observation of a family committed to public service in the most honorable of fashions.

What more could you ask for? A person so genuinely dedicated to public service that he left public office with as much respect as when he entered. In the process instilling that same level of responsible leadership to a son who years later followed in his footsteps with the same results.

To me, there are three types of political public servants: Those who can get elected; those who can serve if only they could get elected; and those who not only can get elected but can also serve. That third type describes to me Jim Norick but with a very unusual twist.

Suffice to list his efforts for Oklahoma City and for that matter for central Oklahoma. Highlights would include the Atoka pipeline and Draper Lake providing new sources of precious water for a growing community and later involvement in the McGee Creek Reservoir.

Add efforts for the first commercial jet passenger service at Will Rogers World Airport which we now assume was always there. Put in a pinch of major highway activities such as the turnpike to Lawton and the right of way for the Crosstown Expressway. As you look at Bricktown today, reflect upon 1967 when plans were finalized for the Myriad Convention Center, now known as the Cox Convention Center.

The list obviously goes on but I pause here to give an important civic lesson. One vote does count. But for this object lesson in the importance of each of us participating in the democratic process, the service of the two Mayor Noricks may never have happened.

In Jim's first mayor's race he came in third in the primary. He was out of it. The runoff would be between the top two vote getters and Jim was 47 votes behind in third place. History? Not quite.

Jim did what most self-respecting candidates who came that close would do. He did what supporters wanted him to do. He asked for a recount.

By one vote. One measly vote. Jim moved into second place, made the runoff, and went on to win and become Mayor of "the largest city in the world."

One vote set in motion this book about two great public servants.

Who among us could have known that one vote made all this possible for our great city and state? What a challenge that should be to all those who care about the direction in which we might be going. You can and do make a difference.

On a personal note, I appreciate the service and the longtime friendship of the two Mayor Noricks. In the most personal comment possible, you can imagine why I was honored that Jim and Madalynne Norick served as co-chairs in Oklahoma City for my campaigns for Governor. You're right; I'm biased but "facts is facts."

I am equally pleased to join my friend Governor Frank Keating in two governors saluting two mayors who made our jobs easier.

—GOVERNOR GEORGE NIGH

FOREWORD

BY GOVERNOR FRANK KEATING

I REMEMBER THE FIRST OFFICIAL FUNCTION I shared, as a newly inaugurated Governor, with the Mayor of Oklahoma City.

It was a bright spring morning in 1995, and I was among those attending the annual Mayor's Prayer Breakfast at the Civic Center Music Hall in downtown Oklahoma City. As a native Tulsan, I had moved here in January to take up the duties of my new office. Cathy and I were just getting settled in the Governor's Mansion, but we were already impressed by the energy and leadership Ron Norick had displayed in winning citizen support for the ambitious MAPS revitalization project.

The date of that prayer breakfast, of course, was April 19, 1995, and within hours after we shook hands and left the music hall, Ron Norick and I would find ourselves thrust together once again on a rubble-strewn street just blocks from his office at City Hall, and from mine at the State Capitol.

Everyone knows the history of the Oklahoma City bombing: the heroism of rescue workers, the compassion of our citizens, the courage of those who rushed to help, and the close cooperation among the many agencies involved. It soon came to be known as "The Oklahoma Standard," and it is a continuing source of pride for all of us. What many people don't realize is that the Oklahoma Standard of linked hands and hearts actually began months before that cataclysmic moment on April 19. It was forged first of all by a man whose father had once served as Mayor, and whose vision for his city was to come true in ways even he never anticipated.

What a delightful idea this book is! A joint biography of two men, from two different generations, whose shared passion for Oklahoma City helped transform it into the world class community it became in the 1990s.

One of my distinguished predecessors as Governor, George Nigh, was a contemporary with Mayor Jim Norick, and his foreword details that relationship. I was fortunate enough to share executive office with Mayor Ron Norick and to be one of his grateful constituents, and I think that qualifies me, on both levels, to assess his time in office. It was simply superb.

We all remember how badly Oklahoma was hurt by the oil bust of the early 1980s, and how Oklahoma City in particular suffered. Those were not the best of years for our state. But like Oklahomans of past generations who have also experienced hard times, we refused to surrender to self pity. We stood up, went to work, and looked ahead. Few could imagine what "ahead" really meant, thanks to the vision of Ron Norick.

During the years following the 1995 bombing, as I traveled outside our borders, people would ask two questions: Tell us about April 19 . . . how did you respond to so well? And then came: This MAPS project . . . isn't that something?

It certainly was, and is. In just more than a decade, Oklahoma City transformed itself from a community some thought was flat on its back to one that served as a model for how to jump start a community. Ron Norick did that . . . not by himself, as he would be the first to tell you, but it was his vision and his drive and his dogged persistence that made MAPS happen. On two occasions, Oklahoma City voters overwhelmingly trooped to the polls and taxed themselves to make MAPS a reality. They watched the many civic revitalization projects reach for the sky, and they applauded their completion. Oklahoma City was getting more than a new skyline; MAPS was also something of a heart transplant, and by the time Mayor Norick left office, that heart was beating with strength and confidence.

The chief executive of any government, city, state or national, has three basic functions.

He should have a vision for the future that seeks to make society a better place for all of our citizens. He should attend to the "nuts and bolts" of daily government, making sure trash is picked up on time. And he should be ready to lead in a time of crisis.

Ron Norick met all those criteria as Mayor of Oklahoma City. His administration, which closely paralleled mine as Governor, was marked by a great tragedy, and by equally great triumphs. Now that he's retired from public life, he can say the one thing every honorable public official hopes to say at the end of his time in office: I left my community better than I found it.

He certainly did, and I am proud he was my Mayor.

—GOVERNOR FRANK KEATING

CHAPTER 1

NORICK HISTORY

BENJAMIN FRANKLIN NORICK was born in Indiana during March of 1845 with a name that was prophetic in terms of what two of his sons would accomplish as a career. His namesake was the famous colonial printer from Philadelphia; his sons, Lon and Henry Norick, were destined to be well-known printers in the young state of Oklahoma.

George Alonzo (Lon) was born February 22, 1878, and Henry Calvin was born April 16, 1893. Henry came into this world in the Cherokee Nation of Indian Territory where the family was renting farm land, having moved there from Indiana.[1]

In 1906, Henry worked the coal mines near Haileyville, Oklahoma. He was 12 years old and greased the mine cars with a heavy bucket of black jack - the thick oil that oozed out of the ground. Henry was stained the color of yellow from his waist down, caused by the oil soaking into his skin as he gathered it. He was relieved to later work down in the mine

Henry Norick bought into his brother Lon's printing company in 1914. Henry eventually bought Lon's share and became sole owner of the Norick Brothers plant. *Courtesy James Norick.*

where it was cool, having grown weary of working in the heat and oil up on top.[2]

Lon, fifteen years older than Henry, was the one who got started in the printing business working for *The Douglas County Herald* in Missouri. Lon went on to work in several Oklahoma markets including the *Hartshorne Sun*, the *Muskogee Times*, the *Muskogee Phoenix*, and the *Times-Journal* publishing company in Oklahoma City in 1907.

In May of 1910, Lon purchased the Union Printing Company located at 310 West California Avenue. He actually traded his home and assumed a $100 debt to acquire the firm. Lon quickly sent word to his younger brother, Henry, to come learn the printer's trade and go to work for him.

At the age of 17, Henry ran errands, fed presses, and anything else needed for the wage of $6 per week. Within a year, the plant was moved to 108 ½ West Grand Avenue and Henry moved with it.[3]

In 1914, Henry purchased a one-third interest in the business for $500 to be paid from his salary to Lon. By this time, Henry was earning $10 per week. This also is when the name was changed from the Union Printing Company to Norick Brothers.

Henry had lived with Lon and his wife, Effie, until February 24, 1917, when 21-year-old Henry married 17-year-old Ruth Coleman. Henry and Ruth took the Interurban from Oklahoma City to El Reno that day and exchanged vows in the Methodist Church. When they returned to Oklahoma City, they moved into their home at 706 Northwest 26th Street. It was in this house on January 23, 1920, that the future first Oklahoma-born mayor of Oklahoma City, James H. Norick, was born.[4]

The Norick Brothers plant was moved to 130 ½ West Grand and took up the entire second floor of the old Overholser Building at the corner of Grand Boulevard and Robinson Avenue. This

The Henry and Ruth Norick family. Henry and Ruth in back, with from left to right: Frances, Dorothy, future Oklahoma City mayor James, and Marjorie. *Courtesy James Norick.*

is where the Noricks hit upon the idea of supplying Ford dealers with bookkeeping forms and other printed materials.

The only Ford dealer in Oklahoma City at that time was J. W. McDaniel. After selling him on the idea that standardized forms were needed, he agreed to purchase the forms from Norick Brothers. Samples were sent all over the state to Oklahoma Ford dealers. The first customer to place an order was the T. E. Gunn Ford dealer in Poteau.[5] "That looked like a million dollars to see that business come in by mail," Henry later told an interviewer[6]

They branched out from there to Texas, then Arkansas, Missouri, and Kansas. Eventually, a mailing list of Ford dealers for the entire United States was acquired and business was good. In 1922, a Texas Ford dealer wrote, "We have been using the Norick accounting system since July, 1920, and could not do without it."

Getting to know the Ford business interested the Noricks to the point that in the fall of 1923, they purchased the Waynoka dealership. Henry and his young family moved to Waynoka to run the business. At about the same time, the printing plant moved to 325 West Second Street and they purchased a Kelly press to increase the production capacity.

Henry stayed with the Waynoka Ford dealership until 1928 when they sold out. Henry and his family returned to the printing business in Oklahoma City. The plant had moved once more, but this time they owned the building and were no longer renters. Lots were purchased at 705, 707, and 709 West Fourth Street for $7,500. A 60'x80' steel and concrete building was constructed on the site by Harmon and Mattison Construction Company for $22,000.[7]

They had relocated by January of 1928 with a rapidly growing business. In 1914, they did $1,200 in printing and by 1928, they were doing $80,000 a year.

Lon had purchased farm land and began to back away from the printing business. Henry offered to buy him out and Lon agreed for $50,000 and ownership of the building and land. Henry paid rent for the use of it.

Lon later remembered that, "During the many years of our association, our relationship was congenial and pleasant, no arguments of any nature were ever indulged in."[8]

Roy Evans, advertising manager for Norick Brothers told how the company began in a shack next to a blacksmith shop. "They both began side by side in 1910," Evans said, "and both were affected by a new and giant industry which was just being born. Norick Brothers became large and grew to a nationwide, you

Jim Norick in his Classen Band uniform. Jim was President of the band and would make music an important part of his life. His leadership qualities were already surfacing in his capacity as band president. *Courtesy James Norick.*

Madalynne King and Jim Norick had their photo taken at the Will Rogers Memorial in Claremore, Oklahoma. Jim was attending Oklahoma Military Academy across the street in Claremore at the time. *Courtesy James Norick.*

might say a worldwide, printing institution because of the automobile business…and of course, the automobiles put the horseshoeing man out of business."[9]

James Norick grew up with an older sister, Frances, and two younger sisters, Dorothy and Marjorie. Jim, as everyone knew him, spent his first three years of school at Waynoka. When his father sold the Ford dealership and returned with his family to Oklahoma City, Jim finished elementary school at Putnam Heights.

Moving on to Harding Junior High and Classen High School, Jim worked Saturdays and summers at Norick Brothers, learning the business from the ground up. His first job was in the shipping department, where he wrapped packages, took them to the post office, and made deliveries. He virtually worked in every department in the plant.[10]

Jim is seen here posing with his mother, Ruth. When Ruth gave birth to Jim in Oklahoma City, she provided the city with its first native-born mayor. *Courtesy James Norick.*

It was also during high school that Jim formed a dance band along with his future brother-in-law, Jack King, and another friend, Jack Welch. Practicing and hanging out at King's house, Jim met and got to know his younger sister, Madalynne.

Jim and Madalynne had been dating steadily and finally decided to run off to Purcell on March 25, 1940, to be married. The minister of the First Christian Church performed the ceremony and Mr. and Mrs. James Norick returned to live in a duplex on 16th Street in Oklahoma City. On August 5, 1941, Ronald J. Norick was born, setting in place a unique father and son combination of mayors for the city of Oklahoma City.

This photo hangs on Jim Norick's office wall. It's a reminder of those days when he rode the Interurban from Oklahoma City to Norman for duty at the Naval Base. The billboard notes the area at the station where the Interurban cars board for the Norman Naval Base. *Courtesy James Norick.*

From the fall of 1938 until spring 1940, Jim attended Oklahoma Military Academy (OMA) with 600 other cadets. He later would be selected by the OMA Alumni Association as one of the first five inductees into their Hall of Fame. In December of 1941, Jim was working full time at Norick Brothers. Of course, world events that month changed the lives of everyone in America.

"Jim and I were at the Criterion Theater," as Madalynne recalls that fateful day. "His mother and father were taking care of Ron. We went out and sat in the car and heard that Pearl Harbor had been bombed. We knew right then that Jim would be going. When we went to pick up Ron, Jim's Dad was very upset because he knew that Jim would be going."[11]

For Jim Norick, his chance to serve his country came on September 1, 1942. The United States Navy was recruiting Oklahomans to help them get the base at Norman up and running. In fact, the need was so immediate that he and those first few were not even sent to boot camp. Jim began his naval career on that first day of September as a 3rd Class Storekeeper working in the Pay Office.

Things were a little unsettled at first. Uniforms were not available. There were no quarters available, either. So each morning, Jim left his house in civilian attire, caught the interurban in downtown Oklahoma City, near today's bus station, and rode south to Constitution Avenue in Norman. He walked from there to South Base near today's Lloyd Noble Center. "Ron was just a little over a year old at the time," Jim remembers, "so it was nice to be with him and Madalynne."[12]

The South Base grew steadily, adding a hospital, dining hall, barracks, and Jim's favorite hangout – Building 92. That building housed a large dance floor. Jim had managed to become pretty good on clarinet and alto saxaphone over the years. In fact, he and some of the guys organized a dance band. When Tex Benecke, formerly of the Glenn Miller Orchestra, showed up a little later, things really got moving and Jim played 1st Alto Saxaphone.

South Base was training for aircraft ordinance and engineering for naval air. The North Base was for training naval pilots. The hill of dirt on North Base was built for testing the airplane guns.

Jim's duty was to keep everyone happy by getting the payroll out on time and accurately. Every two weeks, he and other staff members would drive to the Federal Bank at Northwest 3rd Street and Harvey Avenue in Oklahoma City. Wearing sidearms, they received the cash for the payroll.[13]

When Jim joined the military, Madalynne decided she needed to do something, so she went to work at Haliburton's Department

Store located in downtown. A short time later, the new Douglas plant being built in the southeast part of town began advertising Oklahoma City job openings. This is where she believed she could do something for the war effort.

Madalynne had taken a number of art classes in junior high and high school. She just knew her talents would be put to work at Douglas when she was hired. They were, but not as she thought they might be. On her first day on the job, Madalynne was handed a big gallon bucket of yellow paint and a wide brush. Men would hammer U.S.A.A. numbers on the machinery being sent in to build the airplanes. Madalynne's job was to smear the yellow paint on and wipe it off to make the numbers legible.

The best part of that job, however, was having a bicycle assigned to her while on duty in the plant. That honor was usually reserved for supervisors. This bicycle gave Madalynne access to the entire plant. This was a perk she truly enjoyed and took full advantage of.

As a defense worker, Madalynne also enjoyed the benefit of gas ration stamps. She lived just west of Villa Avenue on Northwest 16th Street, which was about a half block into the wider ration zone. She received the same amount of gas ration stamps as someone living in El Reno. She would use this to her advantage when she later followed Jim cross country. For the present, she used them as the carpool driver.[14]

On January 1, 1944, Jim was assigned to the pre-commissioning detail of the U.S.S. *Chowanoc* in Charleston, South Carolina. Madalynne drove there with Ron and found a place for the family to stay. When the ship was ready to depart for Norfolk, Virginia, and its shakedown cruise, Madalynne and Ron went to New York where Jim's sister, Dorothy, lived. When the ship was preparing to leave, Madalynne and Ron drove back to Jacksonville, Florida, where they wanted to see Jim for the last time before he headed to

ABOVE: Jim is seated just in front of the base violin as a member of the Corsairs. This Norman Naval Base band played numerous dances and performances to the delight of the Naval person- nel stationed there as well as local Norman residents. *Coutesy James Norick.*

BELOW: Enjoying the skills he developed as a young man, Jim performed with several talented and famous musicians as they passed
through the Naval Base during their military career, including Tex
Benecke. They performed in Building 92 on the South Base, attract-
ing huge crowds. This photo was taken in Building 92 in February of
1943. *Courtesy James Norick.*

RIGHT: Madalynne, Ron and Jim tried to enjoy as much time together as possible during Jim's military service. Madalynne and Ron traveled to be with Jim until he shipped out to the South Pacific during World War II. *Courtesy James Norick.*

BELOW: Jim's ship, the U.S.S. *Chowanoc,* saw action in the Battle of Leyte where Jim shot down a Japanese airplane. In charge of ship's stores and payroll, Jim did his duty like so many others and was one of the fortunate ones to return home. *Courtesy James Norick.*

war in the South Pacific. In Florida, over Easter, the captain gave Jim the weekend off to be with Ron and Madalynne. After they said their goodbyes, Ron and Madalynne headed for Oklahoma on retread tires.

In Jacksonville, Jim's ship, the U.S.S. *Chowanoc*, picked up a floating dry dock to take with them. With the unpowered dock in tow, they headed through the Panama Canal and on to Hawaii, taking 18 days to get there. From Hawaii, the ship proceeded to Enewetak in the Marshall Islands, where the floating dry dock was left. Jim was in charge of payroll and the food supply on-board ship. At ports, Jim always got to go ashore with the Captain to order stores for the ship.[15]

Meanwhile, Madalynne had made it home and back to the Douglas plant. She applied for swingshift work in an office job. She kept busy writing articles for her department in the Douglas newsletter. She also worked in the executive lobby running the dispatch courier service. She would send women drivers to pick up ferry pilots as they arrived to fly planes out.

Living in the duplex on 16th Street, Madalynne and Ron had the support of family and friends. Madalynne's mother was always bringing over a ham for them to eat. Jim even got the neighbors to buy Madalynne a gift from him for their anniversary.

Madalynne found a lady to babysit Ron. It worked very well and Ron truly seemed to enjoy it. The lady and her husband would take Ron with them to wrestling matches. Madalynne always knew when they had gone because the next morning Ron would be trying a toe hold or some other wrestling move on her.[16]

The big fight came in the Leyte Gulf. It was a huge turning point in the war. The Japanese were getting desperate and this is where the Kamikaze runs began. As Jim remembers, "It was a night battle. Everybody had a certain job during General Quarters and I was a loader on the 20mm. The fella' that was the gunner was a little bit trigger happy, so they pulled him off and put me on there. I shot down a Japanese Betty bomber plane. It was quite a night."[17] The battle saw much of the Japanese Navy destroyed by the United States Navy.

The war was heating up in the South Pacific. Jim's ship saw action in the invasion of Lingayan Gulf, north of Manila. Once secured, Jim and some shipmates went to the village of Dagupan, where everyone on board ship was glad that he found fresh eggs for their meals.

Halfway around the world, Madalynne was on-duty at Douglas. Sitting in a meeting, she slumped over unconscious. When she awoke, she took note of the time feeling that something had happened to Jim. When she later got word from him about the shooting down of the Japanese Betty, it coincided with her fainting spell.

Jim and Madalynne wrote each other every day. They numbered the letters because they arrived at different times and out of order. Jim said, "I had a little code I used so she could figure out where I was. But she didn't know where the places were. She couldn't find them on the map."[18]

It took awhile for Jim to get out, when the war ended. First, he had to train someone to take his place, but finally made sure the fourth guy learned the job. On December 4, 1945, Jim got out of the Navy at Shoemaker, California. Madalynne and Ron were waiting at Jim's aunt and uncle's house in San Francisco, where she had driven in anticipation of his discharge. Ron was a little afraid of this man he had not seen much of during his first few years of life. "He finally figured out that I was Dad, though," Jim said.[19]

Jim's deep personal feelings shine when he says, "I enjoyed being a help to the country, but at the same time, I'd rather be home. It was something I wouldn't take a million for, but I wouldn't take another million to go back. It was quite an experience. Fortunately, I wasn't injured in any way. That is really something. A lot of fellas at the same time gave up their lives to help us in this free country."[20]

James Norick was back from war and about to embark on a half century of public service.

Jim saw a lot of action in the South Pacific. As a sailor on-board the U.S.S. *Chowanoc,* he did his duty which included everything from securing fresh food to manning a gun during battle. *Courtesy James Norick.*

Jim with his little boy, Ron. They had to spend a little time after the war getting reacquainted, as so many families did who were separated by duty.
Courtesy Jim Norick.

Keep *Young Manpower Working*

James H. "Jim" Norick
Assistant Manager
Norick Brothers Printers

for Councilman Ward 1

 80

(OVER)

Another campaign tool, this business-card size handout was easy to carry around and keep for election day. On the back, further information was provided listing family and background. *Courtesy Norick Collection, OHS.*

CHAPTER II

THE FIRST ELECTION

IN 1946, HENRY NORICK SOLD A SHARE of Norick Brothers to Jim and his sisters. In 1953, they formed a corporation with the same percentages as the 1946 partnership. About this time, Jim became active in the Jaycees, the Junior Chamber of Commerce. Madalynne helped form the Jaycee Janes, the wives of the Jaycees. She and Glenda Phillips, Jim's secretary, named the group, which caught on nationwide.[1]

Vickie had joined the family as a post-World War II baby, now part of that famous baby-boomer generation. Jim had returned to his pre-World War II job in the office at Norick Brothers, handling payroll and other office duties. The Norick family moved into a new house in December of 1949 at Northwest 31st Street and Venice Boulevard. Although he did not know it yet, everything was in place for Jim's entry into political life.

In 1951, Norick Brothers added a new building across the alley at Northwest 5th Street and Lee Avenue. This doubled their square footage and the space was truly needed. Business was good. Jim's family was going strong. His life was in full gear in the beginnings of that prosperous decade of the 1950s.[2]

That was how things had fallen into place one Friday afternoon when press foreman Jack Rainbow was talking with Jim. "Why don't you run for City Council?" Jack suggested. Jim simply replied, "Okay."[3] He went down to the county courthouse that afternoon and filed for Ward 1 in the last hour of filing.

Madalynne had a shop at Frontier City, a new combination amusement park and "Wild West" village north of town, when she got a call that Friday evening. A reporter wanted to verify that "this was the same Jim Norick that's in the phone directory who had just filed for City Council." Madalynne had no idea that Jim had filed. "You'll have to talk to him," she told the reporter.[4]

Jim did not have a campaign office. They gathered at a friend's kitchen in the home of Clark and Chris Horton. To get things officially moving, they put in some phones in the Norick's Club Room. Realizing that he would not have as much time for his job, Jim hired a secretary. Glenda Phillips was a close friend of Madalynne and had some political savvy. Glenda had worked in some campaigns before and would basically run all of Jim's campaigns. Jim remembers it this way, "Glenda and Madalynne – whatever they said, I did."[5]

A few of the plant employees helped, too. They got excited about the campaign and wanted to get involved. They stuffed envelopes and addressed cards. They even marched down Main Street with campaign signs for Jim.

The issues Jim Norick stood for in his first campaign that spring of 1951 were to widen Classen Boulevard, extend Broadway northward, pave May Avenue, and give prompt atten-tion to the Britton Road underpass where flooding occurred and children were in danger of drowning. Norick's business card-sized handout listed his qualifications. At age 31, he had a wife, two kids, and a home. He had been born, raised, and educated in Oklahoma City.

Living at 3201 Venice Boulevard, Norick was in the Ward 1 district of the Oklahoma City Council. He had served aboard ship during World War II as a Navy man. He had been vice president of the Junior Chamber of Commerce, a Cub Scout leader, vice president of the Printing Industry of Oklahoma City, and a member of both the Junior and Senior Chambers of Commerce of Oklahoma City. His job status was assistant manager of his father's company, Norick Brothers Printers.

The election was scheduled for March 20, 1951. Norick was running against several candidates including D.L. Kelly, Ray C. Shaw, attorney Howard Heffron, real estate broker Morris Head, and incumbent Ward 1 Councilman Earl W. Miller.

Two campaign issues took front page. One was the annexation of parts of Bethany into Oklahoma City's Ward 1 and the other was whether to widen Classen Boulevard or not. The people living in Bethany were not all too happy about being annexed and that had an effect on their feelings about the incumbent's status. Miller also was against widening Classen because it would take width from properties on each side. Norick wanted to ease that problem by taking out the center median and lessen the impact on properties on each side.

The newspaper said "Norick has a swift moving campaign." Phone calls and personal visits along with cards and brochures moved the campaign along. However, the paper was of the opinion that Norick and Head would draw votes away from Miller giving Heffron a shot in a run-off with Miller. Norick expanded his political platform to include extension of water and sewage facilities to newly built housing additions as well as replacement of inadequate facilities in older sections of the city.[6]

"I campaigned sitting on the back of a hook and ladder fire truck," Jim recalls. "That was when a friend of ours had an old fire wagon with a hook and ladder. A guy had to sit up in the back of it and guide it and I did that."[7]

The week before the election, incumbent Miller was expected to lead in the voting, but it was assumed he would have to compete in a run-off with one of the three most active challengers, Heffron, Head, or Norick. Heffron had a strong oratorical style typical of the old political campaigns. Head was chiefly in the race because of the property dispute along Classen for widening. Norick had strong backing from young businessmen in the ward.

The day before the election, the papers gave Norick a possible chance based on his strong support by the Junior Chamber of Commerce, their wives, and "the regular anti-Miller votes." They also predicted a high vote count for him because of his "fast-paced campaign of telephone calls, doorbell visits, and an aggressive wave of sign postings."[8]

On the day of the election, polls opened at 6:00 a.m. and closed at 7:00 p.m. When the votes were counted, Norick edged out Heffron for second place and a spot on the ticket in the run-off election April 3rd. Miller received 3,580 votes, Norick had 1,810 votes, and Heffron finished with 1,721 votes. Norick was in the race by a margin of less than 100 votes.

Walter Harrison, formerly the editor of the *Daily Oklahoman*, had finished second in the mayoral race behind incumbent Allen Street. He withdrew from the run-off and called on the other second place finishers to do the same. The second place finisher in Ward 2, Sam Moses, issued a statement saying, "For reasons of economic expediency I am withdrawing as a candidate in the race for councilman in Ward 2." His opponent, Robert Constant, thanked him and commended his action of saving the precinct money it would cost for an election.

Fred Ward, second place finisher from the Ward 3 race, also withdrew. That left Jim Norick as the only one willing to make it a race. He told the press, "I sincerely feel that I have a good chance in the race, and I would hate to have my friends call me a quitter. We have discussed this race and are planning to push it all the way through now."

The *Oklahoma City Times* ran an editorial on March 23rd titled, "Make It Unanimous" encouraging Norick to get out of the race and let the heavily favored incumbent win. Another editorial said, "We regret that Mr. Norick did not consider it patriotic to save the taxpayers in Ward 1 more than $5,000 in election costs."[10]

Norick kicked the campaign into high gear. In one of the earliest uses of television for campaign purposes, he appeared on WKY-TV from 6:30 to 6:45 p.m. in a segment titled, "Why I Should Not Withdraw From the Election." WKY had only basic broadcasts in the evenings in June of 1949. KOCO and KWTV had not even begun broadcasting.

Norick declared, "I've just started to fight." It seemed everyone in power wanted him to drop out. Norick told the citizens of Ward 1, "If the saving of money by withdrawal is so important, why not dispense with election of your city representatives altogether? The processes of democracy are not too expensive. We still have plenty of use for the American attitude of fighting against the odds."[11]

Another newspaper editorial the day before the run-off encouraged voters to get out and vote. It said, "The 36,000 voters in the ward likely prefer one candidate over the other. The margin of the wishing may be four-to-one in favor of one or the other. But unless that favoritism is expressed at the polls Tuesday, there could be an upset." It seemed that the papers supported Miller. Even though there was only one race and that was in Ward 1, city

Brochures were distributed in an effort to get the word out about Norick and his run-off election. With a renewed interest in his efforts to stand up for the citizens, voters turned out to express their opinion at the voting booth. *Courtesy Norick Collection, OHS.*

James H. "Jim"

NORICK

for

COUNCILMAN
WARD 1

Runoff April 3rd

employees were given election day off to vote and City Hall was closed. Norick's camp issued hand-outs stating, "Ward 1 does not want a councilman by default…Americans don't want that kind of dictatorship - or the kind from Fourth and Broadway," which was the address of the *Daily Oklahoman*.

The efforts paid off when 31-year-old James H. Norick was elected Ward 1 city councilman by a margin of 20% of the votes, 3,471 for Norick and 3,096 for Miller. Norick's post-election comments gave citizens an insight into the man they elected. "I could not have won without the help of these friends and their friends [referring to his campaign volunteers.] I have not made any commitments to anyone, other than to promise to always do what I think is in the best interest of Oklahoma City."[12]

KOMA radio's Bob Eastman reported the next day that "Oklahoma City had an election yesterday, an election which proved many things to many people. James Norick, 31-year-old printing plant operator, has been elected as city councilman for Ward 1…defeating incumbent Earl Miller. And in winning the election, Norick proved several things. He proved that the political dopesters…the boys who always know how an election is coming out, don't always have the right answer. He proved, too, that the people, at least those in Ward 1, still don't like any individual, group, newspaper, or organization to tell them how to vote. And he proved, too, that people still like a fighter. In short, he proved that the people still wield a big stick at the ballot box."[13]

Congressman John Jarman wrote a letter of congratulations. He said, "Your race proves our theory that if one works hard enough at actually taking the campaign to the people, then the people alone decide campaigns. We know you will make a great Councilman, Jim, with Madalynne's help, and we sincerely hope that it is but the beginning of a career of public service. Say the word at any time that we can work with you on any project."[14]

A *Daily Oklahoman* photo showed the new councilman with his family. His nine-year-old son, Ronnie, was seen handing Dad his favorite slippers. And so begins the legacy of Norick political service over the next five decades to Oklahoma City.[15]

The caption for this April 3, 1951 *Daily Oklahoman* photo read, "The new ward one city councilman, James H. Norick, celebrated his election Tuesday with a dose of extra special attention from the family. Son Ronnie, almost 10, delivers pop's comfortable slippers while Mrs. Norick and daughter Vickie Lynne, 5, look on. Norick unseated incumbent Earl W. Miller by 375 votes Tuesday and will take office April 10." *Courtesy The Daily Oklahoman.*

CHAPTER III

CITY COUNCILMAN JIM NORICK

JIM NORICK SETTLED INTO THE JOB of Ward 1 Councilman. Of course, there were day- to-day items to take care of, like weed and drainage problems. It seems that between the 3300 and 3400 blocks of Northwest 30th Street in June of 1951, weeds were causing among other problems a growth of mosquitoes. Norick saw to it that the weeds were cut down and the other Ward 1 Councilman, Walter Harrison, joined with Norick to push for the construction of a storm sewer to serve that neighborhood. After the weeds had been dealt with, Leon Hatfield's column in the newspaper read, "And the councilmen will be happy to know that the people in the neighborhood are very happy over the weed cutting that has taken place in the last week."[1]

Norick rises to make a point in this City Council meeting. Seated to the right of Norick is Walter Harrison, former newspaper editor and a City Councilman working alongside Norick. *Courtesy James Norick.*

Next were roadways and rails. Norick wanted the railroad crossings smoothed

Councilman James H. Norick jumped right into working for the people of his ward. Whether it was weeds or mosquitoes, roads or rail problems, Norick went to work for his constituents in City Council meetings. *Courtesy James Norick.*

out in his ward. "An old wail, but sung by a new councilman, was aired at the council meeting Tuesday," exclaimed one reporter about Norick's attempt to fix the crossings.

Norick's first big tussle in City Hall came in September. When Ward 2 Councilman Warren Connor was called to active duty, he was granted an indefinite leave of absence from the council. Connor's wife showed up at a council meeting a few weeks later and was invited to sit in her husband's chair. When Walter Harrison asked if she knew the probable length of her husband's tour, the other Ward 2 Councilman, Bob Constant interrupted and said he had something to present to the council. Mrs. Connor read a letter of resignation from her husband and Constant then asked for Dr. A.M. Brewer to be named as the replacement councilman. Harlow Gers from Ward 4 seconded the nomination. It caught most everyone by surprise.

Walter Harrison felt the council should not decide it in a moment, then offered up L.A. Macklanburg as a candidate. Harrison asked for a ten minute recess and Norick supported that request. It was outvoted by the rest of the council.

Norick believed the council should meet the man, any man, before filling the position. But a vote was taken and Norick left the chamber. He said, "This is the first I've heard of it, and I do not know the doctor. I have the highest regard for my colleague who nominated him, and I probably would vote for him." Norick did not want to vote for or against Brewer without more information. However, the Mayor and five councilmen voted for him with Harrison voting no. Brewer joined the council.[2]

In January of 1952, the president of the Printing Industry of America, Arthur Wetzel, came to speak at the Chamber of Commerce luncheon in the Persian Room of the Skirvin Tower Hotel. This coincided with National Printing Week from January 13th through the 20th. Norick enjoyed his status as city councilman and print shop executive during this week of recognition. Norick Brothers, Times-Journal, Oklahoma Paper, and the Oklahoma Publishing Company all held open houses. A television show titled, Art of Printing and its Contributions to Man was aired. Norick was the on-camera host for the program and gave a brief introduction before the film played. Governor Johnston Murray signed a Printing Week Proclamation in Oklahoma. Norick, as chairman of the Printing Association's Committee, was there standing next to Murray during the ceremony.[3]

Norick had been on the council a little more than a year in June of 1952 and was feeling pretty comfortable with his role in city government. With an eye on the upcoming July 4th celebration, Norick knew the 1937 ordinance against fireworks in the city was unenforceable. He asked parents across the city to help with the backing of the fire and police departments. "Norick, himself the father of firecracker-age children," the newspaper read, "said he will introduce a resolution at Tuesday's council meeting urging parents to stop buying fireworks for their children for use inside the city in violation of the ordinance."

At that same meeting, Norick asked the council to look into the city employees' use of city vehicles for personal use. He also believed that city vehicles should receive tickets "just like everyone else when they park in front of a meter without shoving in a nickle." And he added, "I don't want those tickets fixed!"

Several Oklahoma City leaders, including Jim Norick, traveled to Fort Worth to see the city's new airport. Mayor Allen Street explained that the purpose of the trip was to get some ideas for the expansion of Will Rogers Field. The men were quite impressed and began plans for Oklahoma City's future.[4]

In a July 24, 1952, newspaper article, Norick admitted he was conscious of the fact that he was new on the council and pretty young at the age of 32. He was quoted as saying that he "keeps his

mouth shut, listens, and learns." The reporter observed that Norick was not afraid to say what he thought and had accomplished quite a few things. He went on to say that Norick was "alert and interested and is taking his work very seriously."[5]

One of the perks of City Council duties is to be invited to ribbon cutting ceremonies. Norick, second from the left takes part in the opening of this new J.C. Penney store in November of 1952. *Courtesy James Norick.*

He was so well thought of that in December, Norick was elected vice mayor for the next six months by his fellow council members. His duty would be to preside at council sessions in the absence of the mayor. One of the perks for this position was attending the ceremonial groundbreaking for the $16 million floodway project on the North Canadian River in Oklahoma City. Also attending were United States Senator Robert S. Kerr and Governor Johnston Murray. In February, 1953, as acting mayor, Norick oversaw the drafting of a bill to establish regulatory authority over bus companies in the city, overseeing schedules, routes, and fares.

The summer of 1954 was the setting for one of Norick's biggest council fights. It would be a defining moment for what would be known as the character of this man. Discontent over the operations of the Oklahoma City Police Department had been smoldering for at least six months. On June 29th, headlines proclaimed, "City Council Under Fire for 'Stranglehold' Over Police Force Operations." The very first line read, "Jim Norick, normally quietest of the city councilmen, Tuesday leveled a blast at the council 'clique' that he says has a 'stranglehold' on the police department."

Forty-five minutes prior to the regular council meeting, Norick had read a prepared statement. Then in the council meeting Norick continued, "I noticed in the evening paper last Saturday that a private meeting of the city council had been held on Friday evening and they decided to fire the chief of police. It makes no difference to me as to when the 'clique' would like to get together, but unless all members of the city council are invited, it should not be labeled as a city council meeting, private or otherwise. I was not invited to attend this private meeting, probably because they wanted a unanimous decision of those present, and I am in the habit of voting my convictions, and not the way I'm told."

The night meeting had been held at the Skirvin Hotel and attended by councilmen Bob Constant, Dr. A.M. Brewer, Leonard Dickerson, LaVerne Carlton, Harlow Gers, and Marvin Cavner. Norick, Walter Harrison, and Mayor Allen Street were not invited. The six councilmen decided to ask police chief L.J. "Smokey" Hilbert to resign.

Norick continued with his discourse, "In my opinion, which of course is in the minority, rather than ask the police chief to resign, it would have been much better for certain members of this city council to release the stranglehold on the police department so that it would be operated by the man in charge the way it should be, and not be tied down by the dictates of these certain men. Firing the police chief has not solved a thing. It has only appeased a few who have been campaigning for so long to get the police chief's job. The stranglehold is still present and will be for as long as the old guard is in power. My sympathy goes out to the man who is unfortunate enough to be appointed the new chief of police, for his stay will be measured according to how well he follows the dictates of the almighty few."

Councilman Dickerson, who claimed to have not called the night meeting, apologized to Norick, Harrison, and the mayor for their not being included. Dickerson then added, "I think you have a right to be offended."[6]

It was the beginning of the end for Norick's council work. As in the campaign, Norick had stood for the ideals of the common man and America's basic premise of government. "I'm definitely out," Norick said in February of 1955 in reference to re-election to his city council seat. "I've decided not to run so I can devote more time to business."

Norick and Walter Harrison were usually on one side of issues and the other six councilmen were on the other side. "Most every case, he and I were together," Norick recalls. "There was a certain amount of frustration fighting this block. I thought four years was enough. I had done my civic duty like when I served my country in the military."

At his last city council session, the council voted on annexing an additional 280 acres between South May and South Villa Avenues, south of Southwest 50th Street. Jim Norick was watching his city grow. Mayor Street commended Norick praising his "independent thinking."

"I tried to do the right thing. I regretfully relinquish this spot. I've learned a lot here," Norick added. It would be valuable experience in his future political work. But for now in 1955, he would step aside after a job well done.

Norick had his battles during the City Council years. Normally a reserved man, when his sense of justice was disturbed he would stand up and be counted. *Courtesy James Norick.*

Congressman John Jarman wrote another letter to him saying, "Ruth and I heard with regret that you are not running for re-election. You have done a fine job and a real public service. It is understandable that you would make a decision to get back into full time activity with Norick Brothers but that means the City and State will lose an outstanding office holder."[7]

That would be true, but just for a few years.

Adept at several sports, Norick
made news as a bowler. Joining
his son, Ron, they teamed up for a
father-and-son tournament. Ron
was quite a bowler in his own right.
Courtesy James Norick.

CHAPTER IV

THE FIRST RUN FOR MAYOR

AFTER CITY COUNCIL DUTY ENDED, Norick continued his civic responsibilities. He headed up a drive to provide fans for mental patients at Central State Hospital in Norman. It was so successful that the campaign expanded to include Western State Hospital at Fort Supply. "Funds for Fans" was the catch phrase for the campaign that was especially needed at the Norman facility where windows were small and high on the wall.[1]

Norick, along with five other sports minded businessmen put together a Pro Golf Tournament at Twin Hills Golf and Country Club. It would be the first professional golf in Oklahoma City since 1937. Included in the group of sponsors were hotel owner Johnny Johnson, paper company executive Sig Harpman, Jr., Oklahoma Section Pro Golfers Association president U.C. Ferguson, Jr., former New York Yankee Allie Reynolds, and Maurice Woods, operator of a pitch and putt course, along with Jim Norick.[2]

59

Another sport that Norick participated in was bowling. His son, Ronnie was pretty good at it too. They signed up as a father-and-son team for the Times Classic tournament in 1957. Ronnie was 15 years old at the time and was making sports news with his bowling skills.[3]

Madalynne was busy in the Oklahoma City area as well. Taking advantage of Ronnie's bowling prowess, Mom joined her son in the Southside Mixed Doubles Tournament at Capitol Sports Center. Madalynne appeared quite often in the newspaper as a busy mother, organizer, and civic leader.

One photo showed Madalynne volunteering for pool cleaning duties at the Hillcrest Golf and Country Club. Her Junior Hospitality Club duties saw her promoting the "Fabulous Follies," a fundraiser for local organizations. Another photo session for the newspaper demonstrated her modeling skills as she was showing off the latest fall fashions. The Mummers Theatre benefited from Madalynne's help as she served as chairman of hostesses for the play "Janus." The Noricks hosted a college student from Panama while she attended Oklahoma City University. Madalynne served on the Education Committee for the Oklahoma County chapter of the National Foundation for Infantile Paralysis to help educate the public on this medical disorder. She even found time to begin a "Cookie Exchange Party" at Christmas time, where women brought their favorite cookies and exchanged them. The party became an annual event. Selected as Homemaker of the Week, December 15, 1955, Madalynne's contributions were outlined aside from above mentioned items as: Service Chair for the Camp Fire Girls, Skit Chair for the Board of Mental Health Association, member of a bridge club, past president of the Jaycee Janes, and President of the Junior Hospitality Club.

Jim Norick tended to his business duties as well as the civic duties. He concentrated on running the family printing business

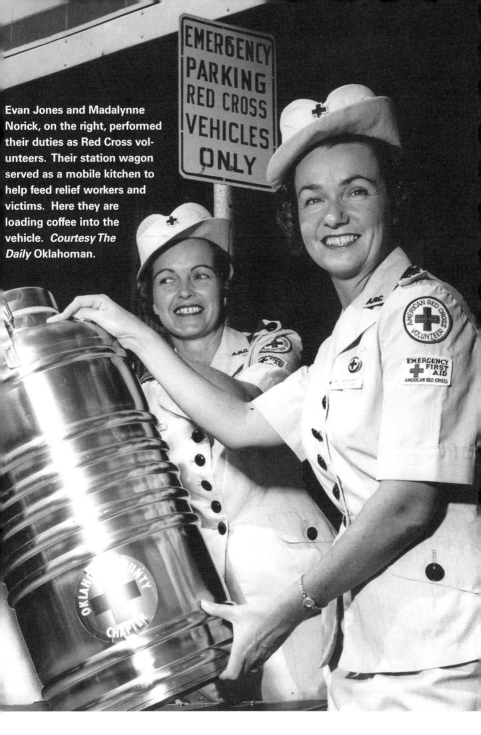

Evan Jones and Madalynne Norick, on the right, performed their duties as Red Cross volunteers. Their station wagon served as a mobile kitchen to help feed relief workers and victims. Here they are loading coffee into the vehicle. *Courtesy The Daily* Oklahoman.

for four years after leaving the city council, but public service beckoned him back. "I was born in Oklahoma City and in my lifetime I've seen our city grow into one of the major business centers of the Southwest. I've learned how people working together as good neighbors can build a wonderful city." This is how Norick began his luncheon announcement in the Skirvin's Persian Room on Wednesday, January 28, 1959. "But Oklahoma City is ready for even greater growth and prosperity. You can tell this from the way people talk and from the way industry is moving in our direction. I would relish the chance to serve and lead my hometown in making the most of these opportunities."

With that, Norick launched his campaign for mayor of Oklahoma City. He promised to push for street improvements for areas such as downtown to Capitol Hill, as well as to Tinker Air Force Base and Will Rogers Field. He concluded by saying, "I would be proud to serve you as mayor of Oklahoma City and I humbly ask your support. With your help we can make Oklahoma City the nation's best home town for us and our children."[4]

Mayor Allen Street had opted to not run for a fourth term. Charles Burba, Ward 1 Councilman, and Charles Tatum, oilfield executive, were the only announced candidates at the time. In a newspaper ad, Norick thanked his volunteer group, "Neighbors for Norick." He added, "My only campaign promise is to tackle each problem which our city will face on a fair and just basis…The Office of Mayor will always be open to every citizen, should you elect me to the office."

The numerous hours leading up to the primary in March, 1959, were spent knocking on doors and making phone calls. Norick and his volunteers were relentless in canvassing the city. During the course of the campaign, lawyer Merton Bulla and newspaperman Walter Harrison entered the race.

Wednesday morning after the election, the results showed 24.13% for Burba, 23.59% for Bulla, 23.47% for Norick, and

15.45% for Harrison. That translated to 9,994 votes for Burba, 9,673 votes for Bulla, and 9,611 votes for Norick.

"It's just too close," Norick declared. He decided a recount was in order. "I'm not blaming anybody for anything," he said, "but you can count on a two percent human error and that would be enough in this case."

With just 62 votes separating him from a runoff, Norick knew it was worth requesting a recount. He filed a petition with W.A. Wilson, election board secretary, who said action could be taken within 24 hours. Norick paid the required $250 fee for the recount. Henry Norick reimbursed Jim for the cost of the recount to show his support. And Jim's own son, 17-year-old Ronnie, showed his support by planting himself on a chair in front of the storage vault at the election board so that the ballot boxes would not be disturbed.[5]

District Judge Glen O. Morris signed the order for the recount. On Friday at 1:00 p.m., the recount began. Norick, Bulla, and Harrison all showed up for the hearing with first place finisher, Burba, steering clear of it all. The recount started and by that first evening Norick had gained 18 votes. Three people would be counting the ballots, working one box at a time. By Saturday, Bulla's lead over Norick had been cut to 34 votes.

Jim and Madalynne Norick kept a vigil during the five days of the 40,000 vote recount. On Monday, the fourth day, Norick was trailing Bulla by only 3 votes when Judge W.R. Wallace ordered a halt in the count while he held a hearing in connection with a packet of disputed ballots found outside of the voting boxes. The box for Precinct 43 of Ward 3 was found empty. A sealed envelope believed to hold the missing ballots was spotted on a shelf in the vault. That precinct had originally showed 66 votes for Norick and 39 for Bulla.

Deputy Sheriff Y.V. Burks testified that he had been guarding the vault since the recount began and no unauthorized persons had

entered the vault. The Precinct 43 inspector, Nell Lawhon, testified that one of the precinct workers had locked the box before the ballots could be put in.

Judge Wallace ordered that the ballots in the envelope be counted. The newspaper reported that, "the disputed ballots could be the key determining whether Norick or Bulla will face first-place candidate Charles R. Burba in the run-off election for mayor next month." The headlines proclaimed, JUDGE DECIDES 'SACKED-UP VOTES SHOULD COUNT, TOO.[6]

On Tuesday, Judge Wallace and election officials reported the official results of the recount. Jim Norick had beaten Merton Bulla by a margin of only one vote. Norick would officially face Charles Burba on April 7th for mayor. Henry Norick's $250 was refunded. Bulla dejectedly announced, "I had a feeling of fatalism toward this thing. Whatever was to be would be. The votes were in the boxes and there was nothing anybody could do to change them."[7]

So now the race began anew. Jim and Madalynne were exhausted by the primary and the recount. Exhaustion had brought them to tears in fact, when the recount results were announced. They were tears of exhaustion and tears of joy. However, they regrouped and with new energy poured themselves into the days before the April election. "It took two weeks for the recount and we got a great deal of publicity during those two weeks," Norick

The caption for this *Daily Oklahoman* article read, "Minor hassle developed at the county election board Wednesday morning when Ronnie Norick, 17-year-old son of James H. Norick, third place candidate for mayor in Tuesday's city election, planted himself in front of the storage vault. Vote was so close among top three candidates, Norick has stated he will demand a recount and his son said he was sitting there so the ballot boxes would not be disturbed. He moved away when his father arrived and the boxes were removed so the election payroll could be tallied." *Courtesy The Daily Oklahoman.*

recalls. "That left one week before the runoff election. Being the challenger, the underdog, coming up like that, got a positive response from the people."

Closer to election day, Burba charged that a "rumor war" was being waged against him. "Primarily," he said, "they deal with claims that I have sold road materials and insurance to the city and county governments. If anyone can prove any of these allegations, then I will resign from the city council as well as the mayor's office if elected." At one point, Norick claimed his yard signs were being removed from private residences and replaced by Burba signs.

The election, scheduled for April 7, 1959, was expected to have a large turnout of voters because repeal of liquor prohibition was on the ballot as well. Campaign spending was expected to be at an all-time high and the recount Norick had asked for created an "unprecedented" interest in the mayor's race.[8] There was nothing close about this election. Jim Norick finished with 58, 648 votes to Charles Burba's 35,682. The headline read, "Norick Parlays One Vote Lead to a Landslide." Calling it a storybook victory, the press promoted the new "look" at City Hall.

At the Tuesday evening watch party on election day, people were already calling Norick "Mayor" by 7:30 p.m. By 9:00 p.m., the victory was clear. The Norick children took it all in. Ronnie, according to the papers, was "milling…with some of his Northwest Classen buddies" at the watch party and Vickie was babysitting a monkey for a couple of the poll watchers. Norick's parents, Mr. and Mrs. Henry Norick were there as well.[9]

The next morning, Robert Hefner, once mayor of Oklahoma City himself, sent a telegram: "You are to be congratulated on your splendid and overwhelming victory. I know about how you feel

The campaign had been exhausting, but the recount just added to it. Madalynne is shown giving Jim support while he wipes his brow after the long recount ordeal was over. They rolled up their sleeves and jumped into the April election with a renewed spirit. *Courtesy James Norick.*

this morning…You are a young man full of ambition and determination for a successful administration and may I wish for you a complete and full realization of your desires and ambition."

A new day had dawned for Oklahoma City as Mayor Allen Street left City Hall after twelve years as its leader. Young businessman James Norick would lead Oklahoma City into that strong decade of the 1960s.

CHAPTER V

MAYOR JIM

SWEARING IN CEREMONIES WERE MOVED from council chambers
to the Mirror Room of the Municipal Auditorium in anticipation of one of the largest inaugural crowds in Oklahoma City
history. Several hundred people were expected to show. The
large turnout was also expected to honor outgoing mayor
Allen Street. A photo in the newspaper showed Street handing
Jim Norick a bottle of "headache pills." The count actually
approached 400 attendees for the swearing in ceremony. Judge
Fred Daugherty asked Norick to raise his right hand and take
the oath.

The first thing Mayor Norick did after his oath was to introduce his wife and children. It was not going to be the last time
that Ron Norick attended a mayoral swearing in ceremony. Jim Norick said,
"I have a big job to do. Former Mayor Street left a big pair of shoes, and I hope
to partially fill them. New members of the council as well as myself should be

On April 13, 1959, 39 year-old
James H. Norick was sworn in as
mayor of Oklahoma City by Judge
Fred Daugherty. Norick was swept
into office by one of the largest
voter turnouts in history. *Courtesy
The Daily Oklahoman.*

Here Henry and Ruth Norick join Madalynne and Jim on his first full day in office as mayor. The proud parents stood behind Jim as he ran for office and shared in his joy on becoming Oklahoma City's first native-born mayor. *Courtesy James Norick.*

grateful at being elected by the biggest number of people ever to cast votes here. I feel that a majority of the people are looking to all of us. I promised that if elected, everything I did would be above board and honest...and for the betterment of Oklahoma City. I'll probably make some mistakes. If I didn't, it would mean that we weren't doing anything. But everything I do will be to further Oklahoma City's growth. We're at the crossroads – or the turning point...I feel some things will have to be done which the people may not like, but give us a chance."[1] Norick was referring to the number one problem they had to deal with, municipal government financing.

In October of 1959, the accusations that had been made in the mayoral campaign about councilman Charles Burba's profiting from doing business with the city came to light. A grand jury had planned to direct removal proceedings against Burba for violating the city charter by selling insurance policies to city contractors.

"I asked and received the opinion," Burba said, "of three other well-known attorneys and they state that I may be in violation of the charter." The charter states that a councilman cannot profit directly or indirectly from city expenditures. "For the above reasons and for those alone I hereby tender my resignation."[2]

Now it would be up to the council to appoint a replacement. The last time this occurred was in 1951 when Councilman Norick walked out of the vote because he believed they needed more time to evaluate candidates. This time, he was the mayor and probably would not have a vote. The mayor would not vote unless there was a tie and with seven remaining council members, that was not likely to happen. Norick did comment that when a replacement was named he hoped it would be by a harmonious and unanimous vote.[3] And indeed it was.

There were times when it was just plain fun to be mayor. Times like when Arthur Godfrey came to town to be honored by the Air Traffic Controllers Association and Norick was photographed shaking hands with the star.[4] There was also the time that the city's V.I.P. car broke down touring visiting dignitaries around town. Norick and three civic leaders were shown pushing it in a ploy to get contributions for a new car to replace the 13-year-old clunker.[5] Then there was induction into the first Hall of Fame at the Oklahoma Military Academy.[6]

Expansion of Oklahoma City was a priority to Norick. In December, the city expanded from 80.51 square miles to 256.51 square miles.[7] By August of 1960, the total was up to 392.672 square miles and included portions of Oklahoma, Canadian, Cleveland, and McClain counties.[8] The next month, an additional 22.25 miles in Northeast Oklahoma County were annexed including four and a half miles of the Turner Turnpike. Mayor Norick immediately called the council's attention to find a solution for additional police protection for the expanded areas of the city.[9]

In a warning to Tulsans, Norman State Senator Robert Bailey said in a speech, "Now they are three miles out on the turnpike and are coming this way." He was working on legislation to limit city growth. "Oklahoma City has enough land to last 100 years even if they grow at a phenomenal rate," he said. "It can't provide services for the newly annexed areas."[10] At that time Houston was the largest city in the United States, Los Angeles was next and Oklahoma City was third, just ahead of New York.

In October of 1961 Oklahoma City became the largest city in the world with the annexation of 42.75 square miles on the southeast side. With 475.55 square miles, Oklahoma City passed Los Angeles by 17.60 square miles which had already passed Houston.[11]

Norick speaks with Cecil Webb near the fountains in front of City Hall with the downtown skyline in the background. Oklahoma City was expanding and they had a young, energetic leader in Mayor James Norick. *Courtesy James Norick.*

Webb,
ber 1960

James Norick took on added responsibilities at Norick Brothers becoming President while also running a growing metropolitan area. His success at his business helped him to oversee Oklahoma City as its mayor. *Courtesy James Norick.*

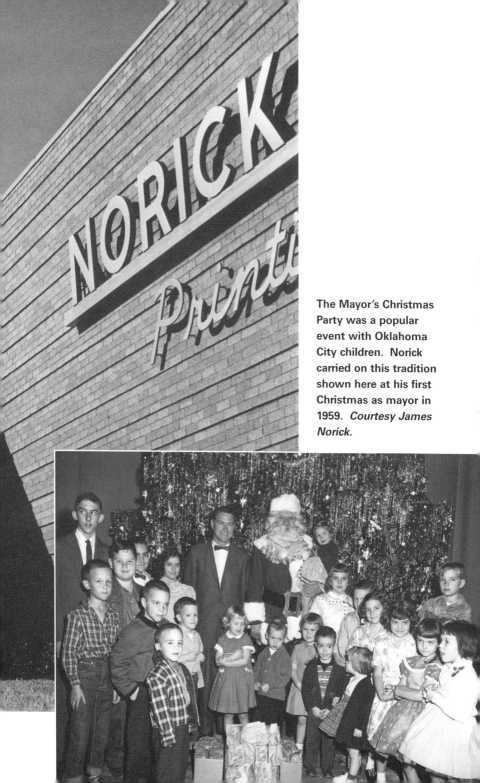

The Mayor's Christmas Party was a popular event with Oklahoma City children. Norick carried on this tradition shown here at his first Christmas as mayor in 1959. *Courtesy James Norick.*

Mayor Norick and the Oklahoma City Council continued to make progress for the community. On November 16, 1959, radar was brought in to help city police with traffic control. A rush to provide sewer service to the new Western Electric Plant on West Reno Avenue was made to help the large facility. During the year of 1959, a record $1 billion in improvements were made in Oklahoma City.

Governor J. Howard Edmondson signs a proclamation recognizing International Printing Week for a proud James Norick. Both men were young leaders in Oklahoma and provided the state with a bright future. *Courtesy James Norick.*

As Jim Norick and Oklahoma City moved into the decade of the 1960s, the young mayor and the growing city were going to see some changes. On January 23rd, Norick turned 40. Less than two weeks later, the first Urban Renewal plan for Oklahoma City was filed with the federal government. Norick's personal life changed as he took over as President of Norick Brothers when his father, Henry, moved into the new position as Chairman of the Board. In February, a $7 million plan to rework the floodway of the North Canadian was unveiled.

There were challenges as well. In March, Dr. F.C. Moon, Jr. led 25 NAACP members to City Council and asked for segregation to be outlawed in restaurants, hotels, theaters, and all other public places. With a petition of 2,000 signatures and the additional backing of the Greater Oklahoma City Council of Churches and the Baptist Ministers Association of Oklahoma City, they asked the city to pass a new law banning segregation. At the suggestion of Mayor Norick, the council sent the proposal to City Attorney Ed Moler. He would meet with the NAACP representatives to work on it.

Moler reported back a week later that, "It is my opinion the city does not have the power to enact a 'civil rights' ordinance prohibiting discrimination in restaurants and other places of public accommodation by reason of race, color or creed. Regulation of matters of this type is not within the scope of municipal government. Such power rests in the state and can be exercised by a municipal corporation only if properly delegated by the legislature. The state of Oklahoma has not granted this power to municipalities."[12]

Shortly after casting his first tie breaker vote on the printing of the City Council docket on Monday instead of Friday, allowing more last minute items to be included, an article appeared in the *Oklahoma City Times* assessing Norick's first year in office. He had attended the city council meeting each week, 52 meetings of the fireman's pension board, 65 luncheons, and 92 banquets and dinners. He made 59 addresses of welcome, attended 21 ribbon cuttings, 10 open houses, 47 nighttime meetings, and 73 other miscellaneous meetings. These records were provided by his secretary, Mabel Krank.

"*It* has been a very enjoyable year. I have met a lot of nice people," Norick said, "and both my wife and I have enjoyed it." He further stated that the vote of spending $55 million to build the Atoka water pipe line "is the most forward step the city has taken since I took office." That water line would provide one of the major legacies of the Norick time in public service.

The early 1960s was a time of extreme worry about nuclear war with the Soviet Union and if Americans could survive it. Here Norick brings in the first barrels of water for the underground civil defense shelters in Oklahoma City. *Courtesy James Norick.*

SURVIVAL SUPPLIES
FURNISHED BY
OFFICE OF CIVIL DEFENSE
DEPARTMENT OF DEFENSE
DRINKING WATER
17½ GALLONS
TO FILL:

TO DISPENSE:

TO REUSE AS COMMODE:

THIS IS A STORAGE CONTAINER AND IS NOT
INTENDED TO BE USED FOR SHIPPING WATER

WATER FOR OKLAHOMA CITY

OKLAHOMANS, ONLY A GENERATION REMOVED from the Dust Bowl, knew the significance of water. A 1954 report made by C.E. Brentz, a city consultant, called for a new water reservoir in southeastern Oklahoma.[1] Oklahoma City bonds were passed in December of 1955 for building the Atoka Reservoir. Ground was broken for this Southeastern Oklahoma lake on April 18, 1958. With the dam finished, the lake began filling in June of 1959, just two months after Jim Norick became mayor.[2]

Jim Norick was a strong advocate for a quality water supply for Oklahoma City. As mayor, Norick provided the necessary leadership to keep water flowing, either from the northwestern part of the state or now from the southeastern part near Atoka.

In the October 30, 1959, newspaper, a large aerial photo showed the filling of the Atoka Reservoir. The new lake rose 10 feet after rain in October gave it a boost. The lake was two-thirds full with about 80,000 acre feet of water.[3]

The reservoir itself could not supply water to Oklahoma City. There had to be a way to get it here and that would be by way of a pipeline. Howard Cudd, municipal bond attorney was in charge of buying the right-of-way for the pipeline and pump houses. That right-of-way was to be 100 feet wide and 99 miles long. The reservoir that it would fill with the Atoka water would be located on the southeast side of Oklahoma City and referred to as the "terminal reservoir."

ATOKA RESERVOIR
CONSTRUCTED BY THE CITY OF OKLAHOMA CITY
WATER SUPPLY BOND FUND 16-1955   DEDICATED - JUNE, 1959

THE CITY OF OKLAHOMA CITY - OFFICIALS	OKLAHOMA CITY ENGINEERING CLUB ADVISORY COMMITTEE

JAMES H. NORICK, MAYOR
SHELDON L. STIRLING, CITY MANAGER
COUNCILMEN
CHAS. R. BURBA   HARRY BELL
MARVIN D. REYNOLDS   RAY A. MARTIN
JACK ADAMS   LONNIE W. SAGE
L. J. WILKES   WAYNE SPEEGLE
OKLAHOMA CITY OFFICIALS
ALSO SERVING DURING CONSTRUCTION
ALLEN STREET, MAYOR   WM. GILL, JR., CITY MANAGER
COUNCILMEN
                  A. M. DeBOLT
DR. A. M. BREWER   WALTER M. HARRISON
MARVIN CAVNAR   CHAS. A. SCHRECK
ROBERT M. CONSTANT
        LEONARD H. DICKERSON
	GUY D. TREAT CHAIRMAN
	HARRY M. HOUSE WENDELL B. SPARKMAN
	GUY H. JAMES C. A. "BUD" STOLDT
	FRANK J. MEYER W. H. STUEVE
	
	C. E. BRETZ CONSULTING ENGINEER
	KENNETH KLAFFKE ASSOCIATE ENGINEER
	
	M. B. CUNNINGHAM SUPT. ENGR. WATER DEPT.
	A. L. JEFFREY MUNICIPAL COUNSELOR
	HOWARD V. CUDD ASST. MUNICIPAL COUNSELOR
	
	GUY H. JAMES CONSTRUCTION CO., CONTRACTOR

ABOVE: Two months after taking office, a defining event for his first administration occurred with the completion of the Atoka Reservoir. There had to be a way to get the water uphill 90 miles to Oklahoma City. *Courtesy James Norick.*

LEFT: At the dedication of the Atoka Reservoir, Norick listens to George Shirk from the Oklahoma Historical Society. The vision for having plenty of water was prominent in mid-century Oklahoma politicians such as Robert S. Kerr and James Norick. *Courtesy Oklahoma Historical Society.*

RIGHT: The new Lake Atoka, a future water supply for Oklahoma City. With water coming from Canton Lake in northwestern Oklahoma, southeastern Lake Atoka's water reserves would help fill in the gap when dry spells hit the western part of the state. *Courtesy Oklahoma City Water Utilities Trust.*

The crowd gathered for the ceremony included bus loads of people brought to the site by the Oklahoma Historical Society. Jim Norick is seated in the front row, first seat. *Courtesy Oklahoma City Water Utilities Trust.*

Mayor Jim Norick in his first year in office. Water was a priority with the young mayor. Looking back on this year, Norick would say that the new water trust project was "the most forward step the city has taken since I took office."

The average cost for the right-of-way was $880 per mile. Five pump stations were surveyed along the way that would be needed to get the water uphill to Oklahoma City. The elevation rose from Atoka at 583 feet above sea level to Oklahoma City at 1,207 feet.

Counties to be crossed by the pipeline included Atoka, Coal, Pontotoc, Seminole, Pottowatomie, and Cleveland. Landowners affected by the pipeline numbered about 360.[4] On April 12, 1960, the City Council approved a $55 million package to fund the pipeline and the new Oklahoma City reservoir near Tinker Air Force Base.

City Manager Sheldon Stirling explained the package in a one-hour presentation in order to solve the city's number one problem, water. Mayor Norick was "enthusiastic" about the plan and it was unanimously adopted by the City Council. Estimates were that it would take three years to complete the project. The 48-inch diameter pipeline would run the 99 mile length between Lake Atoka and the storage reservoir in Oklahoma City. The reservoir would have an earthen dam 7,950 feet long and a new water treatment plant located nearby.[5]

The project was to be financed through 40-year revenue bonds to be paid by water sale proceeds. The water fees would go up about 50 percent to start payments. An editorial claimed this "must rank as one of the greatest gambles of all time." It claimed that a future downturn in the economy would have serious effects.[6] Another editorial stated, "Nothing is more essential to the survival of man than a plentiful supply of good water. Yet few things are taken more for granted until a water supply is threatened. Wars have been fought for water supplies. Civilizations have died when water disappeared." And a writer with the *Oklahoma City Times* further went on to say that they were, "impressed by the soundness of the principle, which is anti-socialistic," referring to it as a pay-as-you-go system.[7]

Walter Harrison added his always unique perspective in his *NorthStar* paper editorial, "Never in history has there been a greater betrayal of public confidence than this financial extravaganza put on by our present council. About the only way a citizen can express himself is to remember the holocaust until the next election and retire the present councilmen as rapidly as they face the ballot box."[8] In a first year on-the-job retrospective, Mayor Norick spoke about the new water trust project, telling reporters it is "the most forward step the city has taken since I took office."

A lawsuit came almost immediately. The challenge in court was to test the validity of the bond sale and construction without competitive bids. At the first council meeting in May of 1960, a group of businessmen appeared to support the water line development. Warren Sherman of Sherman Machine and Iron Works was speaking for the Oklahoma City Chapter of the Oklahoma Municipal Contractors. As a group, they endorsed the trust program unanimously. At the meeting several others stood and spoke in support, including folks from T.G.&Y. and the Oklahoma City Builder's Association.

Hoping to resolve the issues of the lawsuit, a public hearing was offered to let everyone work toward a compromise. The discussions centered on the membership of the Water Trust. At the same time as this water dispute was going on, the Federal Aviation Administration's (FAA) need for expansion got caught up in the challenges. Construction at the FAA of $11.5 million was challenged for non-competitive bids. The significance of the jobs at FAA brought this challenge into play as negotiations continued. Settlement of the FAA challenge came first on August 5, 1960. By August 11, Mayor Norick was asking for a list of names to serve on the new Oklahoma City Water and Sewer Trust. On August 16, the new trust authority was meeting as a group. Two citizen members, Richard W. Camp and R. Lewis Barton served with

City Manager Sheldon Stirling and Municipal Counselor Edward H. Moler.[9]

Almost immediately, the new water trust sought to speed things along by simultaneously searching for an engineering firm for the feasibility study and starting preparation of construction plans.[10] Metcalf and Eddy of Boston was hired to produce the feasibility study at a cost of $20,000. It would be completed in 60 days. The report came back on November 17, citing the project as being sound and entirely feasible.[11]

On December 16, the contract for a 60-inch pipeline to Lake Atoka was let. Lock Joint Pipe Company and Okatoka Construction Company signed the contract for $49,498,839.[12]

A plant was constructed in Ada along the tracks of the Oklahoma City, Ada and Atoka Railroad. The concrete sections of pipe would be built at the plant in 20-foot sections, each weighing 13 tons.[13]

One more challenge awaited the project. State Representative Harold Thomas of Atoka put forth a bill that would require Oklahoma City to compensate Atoka for ad valorem taxes lost when the lake was built. The state attorney general ruled the bill unconstitutional because property of municipalities was exempt from ad valorem taxation. The exemption was without condition or limitation.[14]

Groundbreaking ceremonies for the Elm Creek Terminal were scheduled to take place on May 19, 1961. The day before, Senator Robert S. Kerr, a well known proponent of water, was principal speaker at a chamber forum in the Skirvin Tower. The forum dealt with the topic of the new pipeline.

Another ceremony was scheduled in August when an Oklahoma City delegation of 120 men rode four buses to Ada to celebrate the first section of pipe on the Atoka line. Mayor Norick ceremoniously poured a bucket of water through the huge 60-inch section.[15] Amis Construction submitted the lowest bid for the six pumping stations at $4,749,000. This contract was to be the second phase of construction after the pipeline had been laid.[16]

Additional land would be needed for the new lake near Tinker Air Force Base. The City Municipal Improvement Authority authorized the acquisition of 1,820 acres north of the Elm Creek Reservoir.[17] By April of 1962, the Elm Creek dam was 84% complete.

When Councilman William Kessler cried that water rates would be increased to cover expenses incurred as a result of the new water purification plant, the other council members contradicted him. Kessler had sarcastically commented that if the job had been submitted on a turnkey basis, the additional $10 million being asked for would not have been necessary. Mayor Norick responded, "If it had not been for your friends we would have had a turnkey job [on Atoka]...costing some $55 million to $58 million...Your misguided efforts are largely responsible for about an additional $20 million."[18] Kessler had fought the project along the way.

Contractors were not able to keep skiiers off of the new lake. With 400 acres behind the unfinished dam filled through rain and creek flow, people were flocking to the lake by July. Council passed a one dollar permit fee so rules could be enforced.[19]

Saturday, July 29, 1962, the first official day of water skiing at Elm Creek Reservoir did not go as planned. Rain had soaked the roads so much that no one could get near the lake. More than 150 skiers and 50 boat owners had purchased the one dollar permits to use the lake.[20]

The last joint of the 60-inch concrete pipe was lowered into place near Tupelo in Coal County in December of 1962. The

The 60-inch pipeline ran from Atoka to Oklahoma City to carry water from the moist region of the southeastern part of the state to the less moist and more populated central area. This photo shows the pipe at the end of the uphill run where it empties into the new reservoir on the southeast side of Oklahoma City. *Courtesy Bill Moore.*

pump stations would be completed by June of the next year with water flowing at that time. It would take the reservoir 18 months to fill from Lake Atoka water. The water treatment plant would be finished by March, 1964.[21]

Mayor Norick left office in April of 1963. On July 30, 1964, Oklahoma City Mayor George Shirk dedicated Oklahoma City's largest lake in honor of the leader of the Oklahoma City Chamber of Commerce for 40 years, Stanley Draper. Draper was visibly moved by the honor, offering only a "Thank you, thank you very much."[22]

Three years later, in Mayor Jim Norick's second term, he watched as Mrs. Donald Dunn's name was drawn to pour the ceremonial last bucket of water to fill Lake Stanley Draper. At a ceremony on June 23, 1967, she emptied the bucket into the now-full 100,000 acre-foot lake.[23]

A new reservoir next to Lake Atoka on McGee Creek and a second storage reservoir next to Lake Draper were proposed in a newly released study the following month.[24] Jim Norick again took up the cause of water for Oklahoma City, trying to quench the growing population's need for fresh water.

CHAPTER VII

RE-ELECTION

A NEW ORGANIZATION, the Association for Responsible Government (ARG) was formed in January, 1963, by 100 registered voters to promote five candidates for municipal posts in the spring elections, including that of the office of mayor. With no candidates selected to run, organization president Frank Carey, Jr. said, "All we ask of the candidates is that they feel a deep responsibility to the city and to the office for which they will be nominated."[1]

The ARG was inspired by the Dallas Citizens Charter Association that began in 1936. All funds for the candidates were to be raised and handled by the ARG, not the candidates themselves. Kansas City had just elected a "clean slate" for their city government similar to this initiative. That is what inspired the Oklahoma City group to move forward with their plans.[2]

Two weeks after the ARG formed, James Norick announced that he would seek a

Jack S. Wilkes, President of Oklahoma City University was chosen by the newly formed Association for Responsible Government as their candidate for mayor. Wilkes, a Methodist minister, had been OCU president for over five years. *Courtesy City of Oklahoma City.*

second term as Mayor of Oklahoma City. "The potential for future progress of Oklahoma City is extremely bright," he declared. "During the past four years, the city's industrial, economic, and physical growth has surpassed that of any other period. With proper guidance, the next four years promise even greater gains in all of these areas."[3]

Of the accomplishments he listed, the one that stood out was the land area growth from 85 square miles to about 640 square miles. Some of the major businesses considering establishing plants included General Electric, Ling-Timco-Vought, Inc., and Westinghouse. Also, a $90 million bond issue was passed in 1962 for city improvements. Three reasons Norick cited for seeking re-election were the potential for future progress in the city; the upsurge in the city's economy; and the support of friends and associates.

He said he would not seek the support of the new ARG. Since they planned to select their own candidates, he believed it would not be proper for him to seek its support. Norick set up campaign headquarters at 114 North Walker with C.F. "Tag" Kimberling, the head of a city grocery firm, as chairman of the campaign. Co-chairmen in each ward were B.C. Clark, Jr. in Ward 1, Ed Polk in Ward 2, Nelson Keller in Ward 3, and Bob G. Wilkes in Ward 4. Campaign finance managers were to be Clark Horton and Evan C. "Cap" Jones.[4]

In February, the *Black Dispatch* newspaper came out with an editorial concerning the ARG. The paper said, "…based on our experience in political activities in this city and state, [we] could not endorse such a movement."[5]

The ARG announced its candidates on February 18, 1963, with the President of Oklahoma City University (OCU), Jack S. Wilkes, as their candidate for Mayor. Wilkes said, "We are citizens with a mission. We are willing to run only under the urgings of

P. O. BOX 1942   OKLAHOMA CITY, OK!
MEMBERSHIP APPLICATION FORM

MR.
MISS
MRS.
MR. AND MRS. _____ ADDRESS _____

TEL. NO. _____ WARD NO. _____
ENCLOSED IS A MINIMUM OF $1 FOR MEMBERSHIP IN THE ARG.
(NOTE: IN CASE OF HUSBAND AND WIFE, PLEASE SEND MINIMUM
OF $2.)

I/We would like to help further by:

☐ Attempting to solicit 5 new members, and mail their applica-
tions and money within 72 hours.
☐ Serving on an ARG committee; please call me.
☐ Distributing literature about the slate when it becomes available.

SIGNATURE(S) _____

_____

NO ARMY CAN WITHSTAND THE STRENGTH OF AN IDEA WHOSE TIME HAS COME

The ARG began to solicit membership to help fund their campaigns. Inspired by chapters in Dallas and Kansas City, the organization began with a membership totaling 100 at a dollar a person. *Courtesy Norick Collection, OHS.*

ASSOCIATION FOR RESPONSIBLE GOVERNMENT

the association. We believe the crusade the association has begun is absolutely vital to Oklahoma City's future."[6] Wilkes had been OCU's president since 1957. Born on August 5, 1917, in Honey Grove, Texas, Wilkes was a Methodist minister. He had led an effort at OCU known as the "Great Plan," which was a program conducted with the Massachusetts Institute of Technology leading to widespread recognition for OCU.

So the campaign had begun. Mayor Norick continued in his duties as mayor. He attended a banquet to kick off the fund raising drive for a new southside hospital to be located at Southwest 44th and Western Avenue.[7] He helped dedicate the new Will Rogers Garden Exhibition building at Northwest 36th and Grand Boulevard.[8] He was elected president of Oklahoma City Beautiful, an organization formed as an outgrowth of his beautification committee.[9]

The ARG candidates for mayor and city council jumped on their first issue calling current city leadership ineffective and promised to be 24-hour representatives of the people if elected. All ARG candidates pledged to work full time at their offices to solve the city's needs and problems.[10]

In an editorial the *North Star* newspaper said, "In an effort to offer five new faces the ARG ignored the one businessman in Oklahoma City who has the experience to serve in the office of mayor…James H. Norick. Norick's record in this office shows that for four years he has backed the very thing for which the Association claims it was organized, responsible government. He has supported every move which has helped Oklahoma City progress at a rate unequalled by any other metropolitan area in the nation. He has fought against power plays by a majority faction of the council, which would have set Oklahoma City back in its march of progress…Norick is THE man for the office of mayor."[11]

The very next day, just 30 minutes before election primary deadline, four women filed with the state election board and added Mayor Norick's application with theirs for city offices. They claimed that Oklahoma state statutes call for city office-seekers in cities where more than one county's voters can vote, must file with the state election board. If they were right about the law, then they would be the only eligible candidates for city council and Norick for mayor.[12]

By that evening, the *Oklahoma City Times* headlines read, "Women's Slate Branded Hoax in Council Race." "It's a trick on the voters of Oklahoma City," Frank Carey, president of the ARG claimed. Norick said he was contacted a few hours before the deadline by Charles Adams, a city attorney, who told him about the state statutes. "The ladies wanted me to sign up, too," Norick said. "So I did."[13] *The Daily Oklahoman* supported the ARG in its editorial page by saying that the majority in the council had "ridden roughshod over the mayor and the other three council-men." They called for the new slate without anything negative about Norick, yet supporting Wilkes.[14]

As for the filing with the state, Norick explained that he did it because he found out the information at such a late hour. After filing and then talking with attorneys, he saw that his action was justified in their view. He went on to say that he hoped the attorney general would allow the election to continue, and it was.[15]

Two days later, Norick's campaign suffered a blow when Tag Kimberling stepped down as campaign manager. Norick explained to the press that Kimberling, a food market owner, was a right-to-work supporter and union members could not therefore support Norick. Kimberling stepped down to allow that vote for Norick.[16]

In a paid political advertisement, Norick listed several promises including to work to get the city charter amended allowing the mayor voting and veto powers. This didn't impress *The Daily Oklahoman*. In an editorial they wrote, "…many people seem to be willing to vote for the candidate from their ward selected by the Association for Responsible Government. But they are not sure about the mayor's race. Yet without the clinching vote of Jack Wilkes as mayor, the ARG ward candidates possibly might have their hands tied. The voters of Kansas City did not make this mistake. They, too, had a personable mayor, renowned for his speech-making and ribbon-cutting capabilities…They swept Mayor Roe Bartle out of office along with the rest."[17]

The race had come down to the final minutes. No one really knew how this one would turn out. Would the people of Oklahoma City keep their current mayor or would they go with this new slate concept? At 7:15 p.m. the first votes came in at 231 for Wilkes and 70 for Norick. It was an indication of the evening tally. At 7:50 p.m. the count was 875 for Wilkes and 350 for Norick. By 9:00 p.m. it was 27,000 for Wilkes and 13,000 for Norick. The people had chosen the ARG. A reporter described the scene: "Norick, gray-faced but gamely smiling, had come down the hall to concede and offer Wilkes his congratulations. The crowd [ARG] touched by Norick's gesture, applauded as the two men spoke briefly in the glare of photoflood lights. 'Here' Wilkes told his friends, holding Norick's hand, 'is a great guy.'"[18]

Prior to the concession, the Norick watch party in the West Room of the Sheraton-Oklahoma Hotel held out hope. Three television sets displayed the three network affiliates' coverage of the election during regular programming. In the crowd, several young people wore bow ties to support their candidate. When the 8:30 p.m. tally showed 14, 047 for Wilkes and 7,857 for Norick, the mayor said, "That's it." Madalynne pleaded, "No, Jim. One more return." "All right," the mayor smiled, "One more return."

When the next return came in, Norick said, "The voters have just associated me with the rest of the council. I tried while I was in office. I did my best." He held out his arm to his wife and said, "We had best go congratulate Dr. Wilkes." Madalynne smiled and said, "We'll take a vacation now. We've needed one for four years." A few minutes earlier she had said, "Win or lose, this is the last time."[19]

The final official count was Wilkes - 35,500, Norick – 15,562. It would not be the last time.

CHAPTER VIII

SECOND CHANCE

JACK WILKES WAS SWORN IN AS MAYOR on April 9, 1963. With only four of the ARG councilmen being elected, there were two distinct blocks in City Hall. Constant bickering between the four ARG council members and the four non-ARG council members usually threw the votes into a tie. Wilkes was then called on to cast the tie-breaker. The constant stress of this decision-making or the bickering or both, led to Wilkes' acceptance of a different position as president of Centenary College in Shreveport, Louisiana. Wilkes served as Oklahoma City mayor only one year, resigning on May 3, 1964 to move to Shreveport.

Wilkes had resigned as OCU president two months after becoming mayor to return to the pastorate. Therefore, his resignation as mayor to become president of another college came as a shock to many people.[1]

Now, the position of mayor was vacant and the divided Council faced

Norick heads into the voting booth to cast his vote in the 1967 Mayoral election. It was a campaign to win back the mayor's office and to defeat the ARG.
Courtesy James Norick.

the daunting task of coming together without a tie-breaking vote to fill the vacancy. The city charter provided that the vacancy of mayor was to be filled by appointing a City Council member as mayor. When Wilkes resigned, the four ARG councilmen had a problem. If they appointed one of their own to fill the mayor's job, then they would be one member short and lose their control of the Council. So they had to look for another way. George Shirk was a local attorney and civic leader. He had chaired several committees for Oklahoma City government. Shirk was well liked and seemed to be a choice all Council members could agree with. He was approached by Ward 2 Councilman William Ware to become mayor after Wilkes had left.

There were problems, however. First, he lived just outside of the Oklahoma City limits. On June 16, 1964, an emergency ordinance was passed extending Oklahoma City limits to his house. Then, Ward 2 Councilman Ware resigned. Next, Shirk was appointed to replace him. With City Charter authority to fill a vacant mayor's seat from within the Council, Shirk was appointed mayor until an election could be held the following spring. Finally, Ware was reappointed to his old council seat. All of this took place in just three minutes.[2]

One year after the ARG had been in office, Ray Martin, a former Ward 2 councilman felt that people were disappointed in the new council members for several reasons. Primarily he believed that they did not "seem to understand the people." He said that was evident in the failure of an earnings tax they put to a vote. He felt it would have passed in a different form.[3]

Jim and Madalynne were too active in private life to just drop out of the scene. Jim served as chairman of the Commission on Stewardship and Finance in his church while Madalynne carried on her duties with the Red Cross as chapter chairman for the Office of Volunteers.

In February, 1964, Jim Norick filed to run for the State Senate from District 17A. In March, a group calling itself the Democratic Council for an Effective Legislature had formed. On March 4, Norick withdrew from the race blasting this new group for trying to form a slate.

"I feel such slates are a threat to our basic form of government by the people," Norick wrote to the editor of the *Oklahoman*. "The candidates are picked by a handful of men and promoted heavily by huge financial backing. The slate is, in effect, rammed down the voters' throats. I have seen the power of a slate at work and its potential threat to the American way of life is frightening...I have decided to withdraw from the state senate race. I will not run on any such slate nor will I run against such a slate. Until the voters become alarmed, I feel no one can defeat this slate with its powerful financial backing. I pray that I am wrong for the sake of our freedoms."[4]

J.D. McCarty, Oklahoma House Speaker and Willis Stark, legislative candidate, came out against the slate concept as well. McCarty said, "Fundamentally, a slate carries the connotation that the voters could not make an intelligent decision. This I do not believe. Our government has succeeded where others have failed due to the process of selectivity down through the years."[5]

In July of 1964, J. Howard Edmondson thanked Jim and Madalynne for their friendship. Still hurting from the assassination of President John F. Kennedy in November of the previous year, Edmondson quoted Kennedy, saying, "With a good conscience our only sure reward, with history the only judge of our deeds, let us go forth..."

Even though he was a Democrat, Jim was appointed 5th District chairman of Oklahoma Citizens for Barry Goldwater. Asked why he was campaigning for a Republican, Norick replied, "Because I am a Democrat, but I am an American first. I am opposed to socialism and I am an anti-Communist. And, that's what this campaign is all about."[6]

At that same time, Madalynne and Vickie were visiting Latin America during a 47-day tour. Included in the tour was tea at the Argentina Pink House with Mrs. Arturo Illia. Prior to this Vickie had been active in her college's annual water show at Monticello College in Godfrey, Illinois. She also had recently participated in the Oklahoma City Charity Horse Show. Madalynne had been appointed Oklahoma Ambassador by Governor Henry Bellmon, with the job of promoting the state across the United States and around the world.

The ARG reorganized on December 18, 1964 when non-ARG council members sought to fire the city manager whom the ARG supported. Frank Carey, ARG president, indicated the fight for a new council for the next spring would begin at once. In 1963, the ARG promised to disband after each election. "But from today," Carey told the press, "we are officially reorganized and can reenter the arena." He went on to say, "We're not much afraid to wage this campaign on any issue whether it is city manager or anything else." This was an obvious attempt to threaten the non-ARG members of the Council with intimidation of potential loss of their seats, in violation of the ARG's original promise to stay out of Council fights. The articles of the ARG stated that, "the Association will not be a lobbying group for any cause or for any purpose other than to elect qualified, capable citizens to municipal office in the city of Oklahoma City." It further stated that "between municipal elections in the city of Oklahoma City, the Association shall suspend, hold no meetings, nor urge any position or positions in connection with municipal matters or municipal policies." Jim Norick had predicted they would not be satisfied with controlling elections.[7]

On February 5, 1965, a new citizens group formed in opposition to the ARG. Calling themselves the Citizens for Representative Government (CRG), the group would disseminate ideas and point out drawbacks of the ARG. "I've been in politics long enough to know that when someone finances you, they're going to tell you what to do," said the CRG president Mike Donnelly. "When that happens, the common folk should band together and oppose whomever they [the ARG] select."

"What the ARG is trying to do in finding qualified men to run for city office is good, but their method of selection and presentation leaves a lot to be desired. There surely is more than one qualified person in each ward. This is really what has prompted our action."[8]

On March 7, 1965, an editorial in *The Sunday Oklahoman* reported that, "There has been mounting resentment against this program in political circles in recent months, and the voters will be hearing a lot from the independent candidates the next few days about the evils of selecting nominees to run on slates." On March 15, the *Oklahoma Journal* added that, "Chief topic of discussion in the council races has been the slate method of choosing candidates – actually opposition to the Association for Responsible Government."

The election was held that same month to fill the last two years of Wilkes' term. Shirk decided to run for the office but not as part of the ARG faction. "If I joined any slate," Shirk said, "I'd be aligning myself with factions. But the mayor should be everybody's mayor." This had been Norick's position, but Shirk did not have to run against an ARG slate as Norick had. He was elected and served out the two remaining years. Bill Bishop cracked the ARG's armor by beating his Ward 4 ARG opponent, Hugh Riley, for that City Council seat.

Norick turned to other areas of community involvement including golf tournaments and musical events. Here he is shown at the Twin Hills Twin Ding in 1964 with Bob Wilkes. *Courtesy James Norick.*

In July, 1965, Norick attended the gathering of Past and Present Mayors in City Hall for Oklahoma City Government's 75th Anniversary. Also there were George Shirk, J. Frank Martin, Robert A. Hefner, and C.J. Blinn.

Sports minded Jim Norick served as co-chair of the Oklahoma City Open Golf Tournament. Big names participating included Arnold Palmer, Charles Coody, and Gay Brewer. Norick also was a member of the Hockey Hounds. This was a group of Oklahoma City businessmen supporting the Blazers' hockey club.

In January of 1967, Norick headed up the Mayor's Committee for the opening of the new Civic Center Music Hall, a remodeled Municipal Auditorium. The dedication was held January 22 at 2:30 p.m. and included entertainment by the Junior Symphony Orchestra, Langston University Concert Choir, OCU Concert Choir, and the Douglas High School Choir.[9]

By the Spring of 1967, it was time for municipal elections again and Mayor George Shirk and four councilmen decided not to seek re-election. Shirk decided that he needed to get back to full-time work with his law firm. Immediately, ARG jumped in with their slate. Ray Ackerman, head of a successful advertising and public relations firm, was chosen on the slate for mayor. Among the ARG candidates for the council seats was Patience Latting for Ward 2.

Also just as quick, Jim Norick's name was back for consideration as mayor. "I've had a number of calls from people wanting me to run," Norick told the press. "I'm not saying definitely I will be a candidate, but I am going to consider it seriously."[10] Madalynne was at home laying on the couch when Jim came in. "What do you think about me running for mayor?" he abruptly asked her. "I don't like to go out as a loser." Of course, Madalynne was behind him. A few days later on Sunday March 5th, Norick officially threw his hat into the ring. Feeling that people had become disenchanted with the ARG, he felt he could, "provide the needed leadership" for Oklahoma City. So on Monday morning, Norick was the first to file.[11]

Ackerman kicked the campaign off with a statement that "Oklahoma City was on the verge of bankruptcy" when Norick first served as a city councilman and later as mayor.[12] Norick countered by saying financial records showed when he left office there was a cash surplus of $1,004,212. During his term as mayor, citizens approved $990 million in bonds. No bond could be sold by a bankrupt city, Norick rebutted. He said Ackerman's charges were irresponsible and records at City Hall proved it. Norick also continued his attacks on the ARG with a campaign slogan that read, "Change from slate government to straight government." Of course, this slogan infuriated the ARG who saw it as attacking the integrity of City Hall.[13]

One area that truly concerned Norick was the handling of the funds for ARG. The president of ARG said that, "The ARG will not reveal the source of its funds to candidates." This bothered Norick because of the lack of information on who was contributing money for these certain candidates. Norick never thought the men were evil, it was the concept that was bad. The concept left too much open for manipulation. In a democracy, he felt, voters should have a wide-open election, not one narrowed by a small group of people.

On March 21, light voter turnout was spread among five candidates for mayor setting up an April 4 runoff between Norick and Ackerman. Neither candidate had received more than 50% of the vote, yet both expressed confidence in winning. Norick at 17,685 votes and Ackerman at 17,385 were neck-and-neck. At the watch party in the Huckins Hotel Garden Room Norick told reporters, "I was hoping we could get this all over with tonight, but it looks like we'll just have to wait a couple of weeks. I've run a clean campaign," Norick continued. "I think you'll all agree with me. The ARG has been a little nasty in spots. We'll have to fight a little harder. I think it's time we took the gloves off."[14]

Norick pledged in an outline of his program "Forward Action to give top priority to the completion of the downtown convention center." He also promised immediate priority attention to the Oklahoma City Medical Center, the new Mummer's Theatre, and a north-south Oklahoma City expressway.

The bonds for the convention center were originally passed during Norick's first term as mayor. "I am literally sick that it has not moved forward," Norick told the media. "Completion of this facility will prove a most meaningful catalyst to other great and financially beneficial projects in our core city." Norick added that "No selectors of slates will dictate to me in exercising independent, decisive, and impartial leadership. That every action in every area be for the best interest, growth, development and fairness to every citizen of Oklahoma City."[15] He still showed his obvious distaste for the ARG.

When challenged by Ackerman for not agreeing to a televised debate, Norick responded, "I believe he has already had his opportunity to appear on the same platform with me." Referring to a two hour radio show the night before the primary, Norick said that Ackerman stayed a few minutes and did not remain for public questioning. "But apparently lacking sufficient preparation," Norick continued, "the slate candidate did not see fit to submit himself to public examination with me at that time. In view of his discourtesy to the radio station, the other candidates and the people on that occasion, I see no purpose in providing a platform for him for a public debate."[16] With that statement, Norick unveiled a new tactic of referring to Ackerman as the "slate candidate." In discussing the downtown convention center, Norick used this new title for Ackerman more than once.

Norick answered a challenge from Ackerman as to why only $5 million was decided on in the first bond election for the downtown convention center. "Ackerman is trying to accuse me of helping to pass an insufficient bond issue to build the center," Norick responded. "He knows as well as I do that comparing the original convention center plans, which was fully covered in the 1962 bond issue, with current plans is like comparing apples with oranges."

"Let's look at the facts," Norick added. "When the bonds were approved the convention center was to be built generally in the area bounded by Sheridan and California, Walker and Lee, in the area around city hall." Norick said the ARG City Council then relocated the convention center after he had left office to conform to the downtown development plan. "I still would like to know why anything has not been done in completing the convention center," Norick continued.[17]

The next day, Norick was on the offensive again. He caught a mistake in an ad that the Ackerman campaign was running in the paper. "I would have thought," Norick said, "that the slate candidate and his advertising agency would have been more careful after the ad he ran said 94 Nichols Hills residents would vote for him." As Norick knew, Nichols Hills was an incorporated city and its residents could not vote in an Oklahoma City election.[18]

An April 2 *The Daily Oklahoman* editorial supported Jim Norick in a reversal of the re-election campaign four years before when they supported the ARG candidate. This time, the people spoke against the ARG and Norick won 22,529 votes to Ackerman's 21,711. At 9:15 p.m., Ackerman phoned his congratulations to Norick.

Norick went to the Garden Room of the Huckins Hotel where his watch party crowd anxiously waited. The new mayor-elect was jubilant and, at the same time, tired. In his written remarks was the line thanking Ackerman for a "fine, competitive race." He drew a line through it and did not use it. [19] "Ray has done a lot for Oklahoma City," Norick recalls, "but even today, I hate the word 'slate.'"

With a victory margin of 818 votes, Norick told his supporters, "It is hard to believe that my fellow citizens have bestowed this honor and respect upon me for a second time. I am indeed humble, grateful and pledge here and now to reward them with the finest, fairest, most progressive administration in this magnificent city's history."

He closed the evening with, "The door to my office always will be open to you."[20] In winning this election, Norick had vindicated his loss from four years prior by beating the organization that had

ABOVE: Jim participates in brick chipping ceremonies with Mayor George Shirk to begin the process of a new Mummer's Theatre. This cooperative venture occurred the day before Jim was sworn in as mayor. *Courtesy James Norick.*

RIGHT: With George Shirk holding the Bible, James Norick raises his right hand and swears the mayor's oath of office to District Judge Boston Smith. This ceremony occurred in council chambers on April 11, 1967. *Courtesy James Norick.*

defeated him. But maybe the most important aspect of the victory to Norick was the downfall of the ARG. It was wrong in Norick's view to control any part of the voting process like what the ARG had done by hand-picking the candidates. He felt this threatened the very heart of the democratic process. After this election, the ARG faded away.

The day before swearing-in ceremonies, Norick joined Mayor Shirk in official brick chipping activities to begin demolition for the new Mummer's Theatre. On Tuesday, April 11, 1967, District Judge Boston Smith administered the oath of office to Norick with outgoing mayor, George Shirk, standing nearby. Also in attendance was former mayor Allen Street.[21]

The convention center was one of the first items confronting the new group of city leaders. Plans went before the council on April 18 to build the 15,000 seat arena and 100,000 square foot

114 | Norick: The Mayors of Oklahoma City

ABOVE: Norick issued a joint statement with leaders of the African-American community deploring violence. As the leader of the largest city in Oklahoma, Norick oversaw this most difficult of times in the late 1960s. *Courtesy The Daily Oklahoman.*

LEFT: Former Mayor George Shirk brings a stack of work to new Mayor James Norick. It was an amiable transition and Norick was happy to be back in his old office in City Hall. *Courtesy James Norick.*

exhibit hall. If construction started by May, 1968, the cost was estimated at $20,212,677. Norick said he would urge the council to approve plans and get the architects to work on details. He appointed Patience Latting, Hank Moran, and Ben Franklin, all from the city council, to a committee to study the convention center plans.[22]

The sign of the times across this country was racial unrest. Leaders of the African-American community and Mayor Norick issued a joint statement in May of 1967 deploring any condition or tactic "which tends to divide us or incite people to violence." This was in response to leaders of three civil rights groups warning of a summer of racial disorder in Oklahoma City. Among those participating in the statement were Representative A Visanio Johnson, Representative Archibald Hill and Senator E. Melvin Porter.[23]

Norick said, "According to some people, there may be some tension, but I don't feel we're going to have a long hot summer." It hadn't helped the situation when district attorney Curtis Harris stated that if rioting occurs here, "I want the police to shoot and keep shooting." Police Chief Hilton Geer, when asked about the statement, replied, "That would be our last means of defense."[24]

Looking ahead to the next school year, officials understood that they would have to implement United States District Judge Luther Bohanon's integration order. Among other requirements, Harding and Northeast High attendance districts would be combined. Harding would become a junior high and Northeast a senior high. Classen would likewise be a junior high and Central the senior high. With no plans for busing provided, the court plan allowed students at a school where their race was in the majority to transfer to a school in the minority.[25]

Part of the pleasant duties as mayor was to welcome celebrities to Oklahoma City like when comedy team Dan Rowan and Dick Martin came to town. Madalynne and Jim were joined by Lt. Governor George Nigh in welcoming these special guests. *Courtesy James Norick.*

Other business that occupied the mayor during this time was the retirement of Mabel Krank, the mayor's secretary for 20 years, including Norick's first term as mayor. Norick suggested Esther Tisdal as her replacement. The actual hiring decision would be made by the city manager. Mrs. Tisdal worked at the Chamber of Commerce and assisted with the Oklahoma City Open Golf Tournament at Quail Creek Country Club.[26]

The model of Oklahoma City in the future, according to the Pei Plan, was displayed in City Hall. Part of the changes in store for Oklahoma City was also taking place outside with the opening of a 3.5 mile section of the I-40 Crosstown from May Avenue west

to Morgan Road. Six months later, May Avenue to Western Avenue would be open to the public and by the summer of 1969, the section of interstate from Morgan Road west to El Reno. [27]

The Association of Central Oklahoma Government (ACOG) was having identity problems in the summer of 1967. Several cities were mistrustful of it. Oklahoma City Ward 5 Councilman John Smith said, "We could be creating a monster here which would take over governmental operations of this city." Paul Rice, Bethany City Manager, simply saw it as an organization that "is nothing more or less than its members make it." It is a coordinating body that is required by the federal government for its member cities to obtain grants.[28]

In one of their better times together, Norick, third from the left, with Stanley Draper, fourth from the left, participate in a ground-breaking for a Fidelity Express Bank. Both men accomplished a huge amount for the betterment of Oklahoma City. Also in the photo are (left to right): Dean McGee, Jack Conn, Norick, Draper, William Harrison, Stanton Young, and R.C. DesMarteau. Courtesy James Norick.

Norick had questioned some things in dealing with ACOG, but while in Washington, D.C., a story surfaced about him being strongly opposed to it. He called from Washington and accused city manager Robert Tinstman of trying to discredit the mayor by placing a resolution on the council docket making it appear as if it were from Norick, calling for a repeal of certain portions of the ACOG act. He further implicated Stanley Draper in the scheme as working with Tinstman to discredit Norick. The mayor said he thought the time had come for Draper to turn over reins of the chamber to a younger man such as Paul Strasbaugh. "Mr. Draper long has been serving Oklahoma City," Norick told a reporter. "He has been one of the primary builders through the years and Oklahoma City is where it is today largely through his efforts. I say this with no discredit to Mr. Draper, but I think he needs to rest."[29]

One week later, Tinstman moved on to accept the job of city manager of Austin, Texas. Immediately, Norick called for an Oklahoma City man to be hired. The council members told him they would make that decision.[30]

While all of this was going on, rumors continued to flow about potential race riots in Oklahoma City. Norick said, "The truth has never hurt anyone, but malicious rumors could undo what has been accomplished by many who have devoted countless hours towards solving our problems." He urged citizens not to spread rumors, trying to keep the lid on a boiling pot.[31] That lid would stay on for two more years.

CHAPTER IX

THE GARBAGE STRIKE

UNEXPECTED ISSUES CAN ARISE from the smallest of things in city government. In August of 1969, about 40 members of the city sanitation department drew up a list of demands for higher salaries and better working conditions. A strike was threatened and Clara Luper was named spokesperson for the group.[1] It had been a troublesome summer around the nation. Civil Rights was a hot topic and Oklahoma City was ripe for its discussion of this issue.

City Manager Robert Oldland reacted with a simple directive; if anyone walks off the job, they will be fired. He said Oklahoma City would be in trouble "anytime the city is run on ultimatums."[2] Oldland prepared substitute trash crews utilizing other city workers in the event of a strike.

Sensing that trouble was brewing, a special meeting was called with the City Council, city manager, and Mayor Norick. They backed Oldland's stand. He had made the

Norick, restricted by city guidelines on salary increases, worked to end the strike with a peaceful resolution. Obviously, there was more to these proceedings than just the question of a raise. Working under these trying circumstances, Norick helped keep the city from turning into a battleground. *Courtesy James Norick.*

working condition changes requested, but salary changes could not be made for just one city department.[3] Salary levels were across the board as far as city pay scales were concerned. Any changes would have to be city wide and not just for sanitation jobs.

Luper demanded a meeting with Oldland. He refused saying that she cannot be a spokesman or representative of city workers

City Manager Robert Oldland is seen standing at the microphone on the far right addressing the sanitation workers. The media was also keeping an eye on this developing problem in August of 1969. *Courtesy The Daily Oklahoman.*

without herself being an employee. An all-night marathon of talks at several locations failed to avert the strike.[4]

More than 200 strikers led by Luper were prevented from entering City Hall by Oklahoma City police. "You have seen the strong arm of bigotry," Luper told the strikers. "I think we need to go right down here to the police station and see the chief." She then led the strikers down to the police station where she and two others were admitted to the chief's office. Re-emerging, Luper said she had not received an apology. She told the strikers to go to their yards where they worked, pick up their checks "and blow the horns on your cars to let the people of Oklahoma City know who you are."[5]

Calling the strike illegal, Oldland began termination of the employees. City Councilman Nelson Keller felt they should stand firm on the strike firings.[6] Mayor Norick appointed a citizens

These men were circling City Hall with signs of support for striking sanitation workers. City Manager Robert Oldland was an obvious target of their complaints. *Courtesy The Daily Oklahoman.*

committee to seek a resolution to the strike. They recommended a $40 monthly pay raise for city workers on September 1 with another $20 on January 1, 1970.[7]

Luper said they would not negotiate down from the original $100 raise they demanded. Then she notified strikers that she was returning to her job as history teacher at Northwest Classen and would no longer lead them.[8] Nine days into the strike, Norick and Oldland met with the new leadership, hoping to resolve the problem. The city council voted to support the study of a pay raise recommended by the citizens committee. The strikers voted to not go back to work until everyone was given his job back. Several positions had been filled during the strike and Oldland said they would not be available.[9]

Oldland reported after meeting with Mayor Norick and the strikers representatives that he would not rehire those actively involved in the strike, including those arrested for blocking the garbage trucks.[10] Meeting with the strikers on the 15th day of the strike, Norick came away with little optimism for a settlement. "We tried as best we could to get our position across," Norick said at the time, "but apparently we didn't succeed. This group apparently didn't understand what we were trying to tell them." Norick called a special session of the city council on Friday.[11] At that meeting, a final pay plan was passed giving a 5% raise effective October 3. Patience Latting and Dr. A.L. Dowell voted against the plan, wanting the original proposal made by the citizens committee.[12]

The strike was gaining national interest. Reverend Ralph Abernathy flew into town to march on city hall. Oldland would meet with Abernathy, Dr. Dowell and Reverend W.K. Jackson, but not with the entire group. Abernathy would not meet without the group and called Oldland's actions a "definite insult."[13]

"I've been jailed 28 times fighting for the rights of my people," Abernathy told an audience at St. John's Baptist Church. "I'm ready to go the twenty-ninth time right here in Oklahoma City." He said he "came here to Oklahoma City to tell that city manager pharaoh to let the sanitation workers go free, to tell that mayor pharaoh to let my people go."[14] It was a sanitation strike in Memphis that brought Martin Luther King, Jr. to Tennessee where he was killed by an assassin a year earlier. Abernathy had taken over the duties of leading these walkouts nationwide after Dr. King's death.

The leaders of the sanitation strike called for a new walkout by those who had returned to the job. Many had families to feed and could not afford to stay off the job, let alone take the chance of being fired. Several workers had returned and yet with the reassignments and new hires, trash pickup was far from being back to normal. People were not paying their garbage fees and trash was piling up around the city. State Representative Archibald Hill, the new chairman of the group, announced plans for the walkout

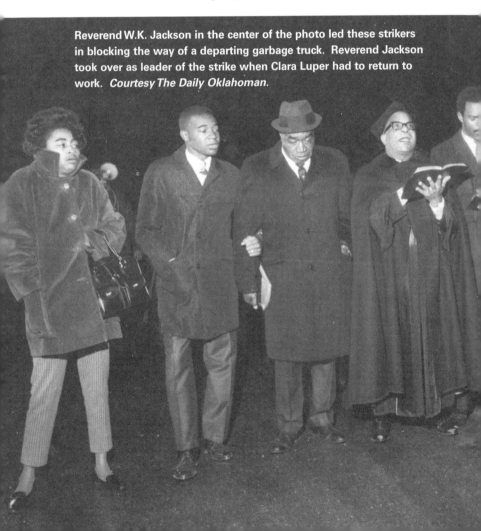

Reverend W.K. Jackson in the center of the photo led these strikers in blocking the way of a departing garbage truck. Reverend Jackson took over as leader of the strike when Clara Luper had to return to work. *Courtesy The Daily Oklahoman.*

and told workers that "all that remain on the jobs will be labeled 'Uncle Toms.'"[15]

With police on duty at sanitation yards and Oldland's declaration that if anyone walked off this time, they would be fired and not rehired, the walkout was aborted. Eight demonstrators blocking garbage trucks were arrested.[16] According to interviews with some of the workers, they did not want another strike and were happy with the raise. Most felt a new strike would not materialize. The workers continued to drive their trucks as protestors became more radical. They feared for their families and themselves, but they carried on.[17]

Dr. Abernathy was expected to help in a "Black Friday" event. Black students were asked to boycott school, and black adults were asked to not go to work.[18] Reverend T.Y. Rogers of Atlanta, Georgia, told an audience of 350 at St. John's, "If there are black people in this city who think they must slip out and go to work Friday, then they better not let the rest of us who are in the streets see them."[19] It was a stressful time for both blacks and whites in Oklahoma City.

Mayor Norick tried several times on Thursday to

meet with the leaders to try to head off Black Friday. Finally, in a late-night declaration, he called for a state of emergency in limited areas of the city. These areas primarily were city buildings and facilities. The declaration allowed police to make arrests in those areas without waiting for an infraction of the law. Norick explained the events to Governor Dewey Bartlett in a 9:15 p.m. call made by the governor.[20]

Reverend Ralph Abernathy led this march of support for the striking sanitation workers. They moved along Northeast Second Street toward City Hall, passing in front of several landmark structures along the way. *Courtesy The Daily Oklahoman.*

When District Attorney Curtis P. Harris filed felony "riot" charges against four of the leaders, Clara Luper spoke out and said it was another way "our leaders suffer intimidation." She named Norick, Oldland, and councilmen Cook, Franklin, and Smith as "professional bigots."[21] Oldland's firing would now be added to the list of demands for ending the garbage strike.[22]

Black Friday turned out peaceful as more than 1,500 people marched to City Hall. Police kept watch as the march remained calm. Norick had given a last minute "no arrest" order and it saved the day.[23]

Norick, Franklin, Cook, and Smith appeared at a press conference and announced a firmer stand against the strikers, as well as a possible ouster of Dr. Dowell from the council. Dowell had been convicted of income tax evasion. Governor Bartlett, sensing another serious round of discussions, cancelled a California trip and offered the Governor's Mansion as a neutral site for talks.[24] On November 2, talks began. Hopes ran high until on the third day when they broke off as neither side would yield on the rehiring of eleven strike leaders.[25]

As negotiations continued, 100 residents signed up for volunteer garbage pick-up duty. Suddenly, after 80 days of turmoil, mediators found success and a settlement was reached.[26] Oklahoma City Chamber of Commerce president Stanton Young had arranged for the 11 strike leaders to find outside employment. This was a key issue and a sticking point. The city would not budge on not rehiring them and the strike organizers insisted these men have jobs.

When the strike ended, most all demands had been met. The strike supporters gathered and sang "We Shall Overcome." Clara Luper asked the group, "Do you love everybody?" "Yes!" they shouted. She asked if they loved the strike leaders, City Manager Oldland, and Mayor Norick? "Yes!" was their reply.

Governor Dewey Bartlett congratulated the leaders and said, "Both sides have been willing to give and to take in resolving their differences. All this speaks well for Oklahoma and for Oklahoma City."[27]

When it was all over and the city reflected on what had transpired, the Gridiron Banquet presented it's annual show. This one was titled, "Dissents…and Non-Scents of 1969 – or – Nobody Nose the Garbage We've Seen."

Leadership had provided the necessary ingredients at the right time to prevent violence seen in other cities across the nation. Both sides showed remarkable restraint and worked to see a peaceful solution to one of Oklahoma City's smelliest problems.

CHAPTER X

THE NEXT GENERATION

AFTER TWELVE YEARS IN PUBLIC OFFICE, Jim Norick decided not to seek re-election. He summed up his public service in the following press release issued January 22, 1971.

Reminiscing over the past 20 years – 12 of which I've spent in public office – recalls a host of gratifying human experiences as well as those related directly to community service.

One incident which relates to both areas occurred in the 1959 election, my first race for the mayor's office after four years as councilman. There were several candidates and the primary was so divided that I squeaked by with a one-vote majority, on a recount of the ballots, to get into the run-off. So, ultimately winning in the run-off was indeed gratifying.

Madalynne and Jim Norick spent eight days in Israel in 1970. Jim was one of eleven mayors invited by the Israel Ministry of Tourism to visit their country. *Courtesy The Daily Oklahoman*.

Several other satisfying experiences during that first term included some very effective future planning by the Council and the Chamber of Commerce which resulted in an extensive Oklahoma City annexation program. The program since has been responsible for orderly development of industrial,

**Mayor James Norick conducting the Symphony
at the 1967 State Fair of Oklahoma.** Norick's love
of music followed him throughout his career.
Courtesy James Norick.

commercial and residential areas and has provided
property owners with unprecedented protection of
their property values.

An interesting side effect of the annexations was
the fact that until a year or so ago when Jacksonville,
Florida entered into a similar program, Oklahoma
City embraced the largest land area of any city in
the world.

Also during that first term, the citizens of
Oklahoma City approved the largest improvement
bond issues in the city's history until that point.
Further, the Atoka Water Project was initiated and,
although there was much controversy at the time, I
think most of our people now are happy with our
water supply and with the added industry and pay-
rolls made possible by ample water reserves.

My subsequent defeat by the ARG in the 1963
election was rather a bitter pill to swallow. But that disappointment
was forgotten when in 1967 the voters rejected the ARG candidate
and returned me to office. It's gratifying to think that this incident
may have put an end – at least for a few years – to special interest
slates of candidates for municipal offices.

Since there's very little financial renumeration for the mayor, the
pleasant memories and the privilege of having a part in the city's
achievements are the important compensations.

There also are some nuisance values. I recall one still night in
1960 when Madalynne and I were fast asleep. At 3:30 a.m. the
phone rang which wasn't exactly unusual except that this was a call
from Honolulu. An apparently affluent resident of that island city

had the hobby – in which she usually indulged after a bit of more convivial indulging – of calling the mayors of various cities simply to chat. And on that night at that most unprofessional hour, it was my turn to become acquainted with the Honolulu lady who liked talking with Mayors.

But that same year, on the compensating side, Madalynne and I were privileged to a private tour of the White House, and to have lunch at the President's mess. This really was a gratifying experience that we'll always remember.

Results of another incident in 1968 were quite happy in spite of the fact that I could have been jeopardizing my happy home life at the outset. Madalynne and I were all set to accompany a Shrine tour of Hawaii when I cancelled our reservations in order to act as chairman of the campaign for the city's biggest improvement bond campaign in our history.

A previous effort had met with defeat of all issues except those related to improving our Fire Department. Many of our citizens believed that Oklahoma Cityans would support all the measures if given another opportunity if all the benefits to the community were presented effectively.

At the time, the assignment looked like a tough one. The total issue represented over $110 million. But I took the job because, in addition to several other important improvements, I was especially interested in seeing the Allen Street Memorial Convention Center get underway. The bond issue during my first administration had made possible the planning and the site, but the 1968 issue was necessary to build the project which later was named the Allen Street Memorial Myriad.

The issue carried, and because of the solid efforts of hundreds of Oklahoma Cityans had accomplished the job, I felt more than compensated for the chore of chairman. And, in view of the victory, Madalynne forgave me for canceling our Hawaiian excursion.

Later that year, we had a rather harrowing experience when we arrived in Washington, D.C. a day early for a meeting of the National League of Cities. The first of the terrible riots that wracked the Capitol City had started just an hour before it fell our lot to arrive right in the middle of the area.

Once we were out of the mess, I felt a surge of gratefulness that Oklahoma City was blessed with citizens who don't believe in riots and this awful destruction of lives and property.

There were, of course, many other experiences and some of the major ones occurred during the year just past. Last Spring, we were privileged with eleven other American Mayors and their wives to tour Israel as guests of the Israeli government.

We'll never forget the tour and our hosts treated us splendidly. But we couldn't help feeling grateful that we are Americans.

Last Fall, too, was a time to be grateful for a side benefit of my office when, in Rome, it was our privilege to enjoy a private audience with the Pope. Although we are not Catholic, the experience was inspiring and unforgettable.

And another incident I'll never forget was a call I received a few days before this past Christmas. Just 15 minutes before Madalynne and I were to leave for the airport to fly to Atlanta for a National League of Cities meeting, the phone rang. A young girl wanted a Santa Claus for her little sister who was dying. The youngster explained that her little sister probably wouldn't live until Christmas and she knew the mayor could find a Santa for her.

Well, finding him suddenly became the most important requirement of my office. And fortunately, I did find him in the person of a long time friend who was happy to take the job and whose proportions made his performance believable.

Those and many others are incidents I probably never would have experienced had I not been privileged to serve two terms as Mayor of Oklahoma City and one term as City Councilman. I'm humbly grateful for the privilege and I shall miss similar experiences in the future.

However, in view of a need to devote more time to the operation of my own business, I have decided that I will not be a candidate for re-election.

Through the years, the office of mayor has required more and more time as the city and its agencies have grown. The mayor is also a trustee of the City's Transportation and Parking Authority and Chairman of the Fireman's Pension Board. He is either directly or indirectly involved with the activities of Urban Renewal, Public Housing and ACOG. He is a member of the State Fair Board and a director of the Chamber of Commerce. And this, of course, is as it should be, but these activities plus the day-to-day requirements of the office and the Council meetings consume the mayor's time.

Now, with the demands of an expanded private business, Norick Brothers, Inc., for which we established an additional Branch Office in Atlanta in October, I feel compelled to withdraw from public office.

However, as a native Oklahoma Citian, I shall continue to devote as much time as possible to civic functions for the growth and betterment of this City. It's a wonderful place to live and to work and I will always do my best to help keep it so.

To all my friends and supporters, my co-workers, and to all the fine people of Oklahoma City, and especially my family, I wish to say thank you, most sincerely, for allowing me to serve two terms as your mayor. Together, I believe we have contributed substantially to the welfare and the growth of the community, and I am grateful for the privilege and the opportunity to serve.[1]

At his last council meeting as mayor on April 13, 1971, council members surprised Norick with a resolution naming the fairgrounds arena as the "Jim Norick State Fairgrounds Arena." A reporter with *The Daily Oklahoman* wrote, "His voice shook with emotion as he accepted the honors and he had to pause at least once to wipe tears from his eyes." Then Patience Latting was sworn in as Oklahoma City's first female mayor. The plaque at the arena was unveiled on June 21, 1972.

A decade later, Ron Norick would pick up where his father left off. The legacy of the Norick name had only just begun.

CHAPTER XI

THE CHARACTER OF RON NORICK

THE CHARACTER OF A MAN IS SHAPED BY HIS SURROUNDINGS and the lessons learned growing up. Ron Norick had wonderful role models in his family and life experiences that prepared him for the challenges ahead.

At the age of 11, Ron decided that he wanted to earn his own money. The Bowlarena on 32nd Street and North May Avenue used manual pin setters and Ron found out he could get a job making 7 cents per game as a pin setter. When he asked his Mom if he could work at the bowling alley, she told him absolutely not. The bowling alley had what she considered to be "some pretty scroungy-looking old men" hanging around it. Some of these men who worked as pin setters were even sleeping in the back room of the bowling alley and she did

This is Ron Norick's senior photo, Class of 1959, at Northwest Classen High School in Oklahoma City. Sports were a big part of Ron's school years and helped shape the man in competitiveness and fair play. *Courtesy Ron Norick.*

not want him anywhere near there. But Ron had already made up his mind. He immediately went back to the bowling alley and took the job. It was about a week before his

Ron, second from left, was a smart businessman and entrepreneur even as a young boy. Here, in 1951, he is seen working a fireworks stand. *Courtesy Ron Norick.*

folks figured out he was working there, but by then his Dad had accepted it. In fact, he kind of liked the idea of his son's work ethic at such an early age. From that time on, Ron always worked because he wanted to earn his own money and be his own man.[1]

Over the next few years, Ron went from setting pins to becoming the janitor up front. He swept the floor, and in between the leagues he picked up all the bottles and cups, then swept out the pits quickly before the next league arrived. Ron was sort of the "houseboy" and he really enjoyed the responsibility.

It was not too long after that when his uncle, Jack King, started running the snack bar in the bowling alley. When Jack took over, he had Ron in the snack bar helping him on busy weekends. Ron could not reach the counter yet, so he had to work in the back as a dishwasher or peel potatoes for hash browns. Once while peeling potatoes, he whacked the top of his thumb off. Ron remembered getting real light-headed and after being bandaged went right back to his work. He never did find that piece of his thumb. To this day, he wonders if someone got something extra in their hash browns.

Ron also ended up being trained as a mechanic for the automatic pin-setting machine. All of this work-related experience was happening to a young man who was still in junior high school. In the evenings, he would get to the alley about 5:30 p.m., and the leagues would start about 6:15 p.m.. He would work until they were over, usually about 11:30 p.m., three or four nights a week.

While working as a mechanic on the pin-setter, Ron would be in the back area. That allowed him to take his school books to work and study as long as nothing broke down. If a bell went off, signifying that the machine had stopped, he would put down his book, fix the machine, and continue studying.

It was not long after that he was promoted to working the desk, where he handed out shoes to the bowlers, assigned lanes, and collected fees. The bowling alley had a pro shop, so naturally Ron worked there and learned how to measure and drill bowling balls. During college, using this experience, he became weekend manager at Highlander Lanes while at the same time working during the week at Norick Brothers.

At the age of 10, Ron began his career at Norick Brothers. He was office boy during the summer, and would go down to the office for a couple of hours a day with his dad. The business was on Northwest 4th Street and Shartel Avenue in those days, and Mildred Gibson was the office manager. She would have Ron run errands for her. Sometimes he would even get to go back in the shipping department and wrap boxes. It was a lot of responsibility for such a young man. But this was just the first step of learning the printing business from the ground floor up.[2]

The summer he was 14, Ron went to work in the plant. Wilson Meek, the letter press foreman at the time, was his first boss at Norick Brothers. Wilson taught young Ron how to run an envelope press, and he loved it. It was a fast machine, and Ron could run 80,000 envelopes a shift. As a teenager, this enterprising young man was going to school all day and working afternoons at Norick Brothers.

During the summer of 1958, the summer before his senior year in high school, Ron worked with Bud Burnell, who turned out to be one of Ron's very best friends and who passed away during Ron's first term in office. They spent the entire summer in a two-ton truck, moving things from the old plant to the new one on Northwest 36th Street, just west of Portland Avenue. They hauled two or three loads a day, all summer long, moving everything except the heavy presses. Bud Burnell later became collator foreman and assistant plant superintendent at Norick Brothers.

When Ron was in college at Oklahoma City University, he went to school from 7:00 a.m. until 11:30 a.m., and then went to work at Norick Brothers. He worked in the mail room for a while, where his task was to assist in the bulk mailing part of the business. He sent out thousands of catalogs and sample forms to Norick Brothers' extensive mailing list. They used the old address-a-graph machines, complete with metal plates, mailing several hundred thousand pieces of mail each year. Some of the mailings would have eight or ten inserts in them, such as return

Christmas with the family. Left to right: Vickie, Ron, and Madalynne hang the stockings by the fireplace. As a teenager, Ron worked, went to school, and enjoyed his family. *Courtesy James Norick.*

envelopes and order forms. The year Ron spent in the mail room proved to be valuable for his future. He became familiar with all of the forms Norick Brothers sent out and watched the incoming mail to see how effective the mailings were. This was invaluable experience for a young man on his way up the ladder.

Probably the best part about working in the mail room was the fact that Ron experienced just about every aspect of the job. He made the metal address plates, as well as making corrections on addresses, firms, and names. Most of Norick Brothers' business was with car dealers, especially Ford dealerships. They could not afford to have salesmen calling in many of the small towns around the country, so the Noricks would send out mailings with samples of their forms. Norick serviced about 18,000 customers who were called "active customers." But counting all of the car dealers across the country as possible customers, there were about 28,000 customers. At that time, just about every little town in America had a Chevy or Ford dealer in it, so it really helped him learn who their active customers were.[3]

The next step in young Ron's career was in computers. In 1962, he started the first automated system inside Norick Brothers from scratch. They acquired a Univac 1004, which Ron programmed himself. He wrote the programs, prepared the flow-charts and even hard-wired all the panels into the circuit boards. They automated their payroll, production schedules, and billings with key-punched cards. In fact, Ron wrote his senior thesis in the fall of 1963 at OCU on the Univac 1004 computer, which was revolutionary for the time. He stayed with the computer department for more than three years, learning the different job classifications and profit centers at Norick Brothers.[4]

Next in Ron's business life was cost accounting and estimating. Ron was chief estimator for more than four years, which allowed him to work with all the salesmen. Those salesmen would look for Ron when they called in with custom jobs, because Ron had developed a price book and was able to quickly give them a price quote for any job.

By 1971, the Norick Brothers' business had really started growing. They were running two shifts and things were going well. Because Ron had worked in the plant, the mail room, the computer room, and the estimating end of the business, he had acquired a strong knowledge of the equipment, what it could do, what the costs were, and how the business worked. So Norick Brothers, Inc. created a new position, vice president of manufacturing, and promoted Ron into that position.

By the time Ron became vice president of manufacturing, Norick Brothers employed approximately 200 people. Ron had been working at the company from the time he was 10 years old, including 6 years in the plant, and had done everything from setting type to shoveling lead, from running the collators and working in the mail room to working in the press room. He literally had done it all and the other employees recognized that he knew the business. He always had respect for the employees and the job they performed, whatever it was, and they in turn had respect for him. Ron could walk through the plant, calling every employee by name, whether they were sweeping the floor or working on the presses, and they would smile and call him "Ron" right back. He was treated as an employee and not the owner's son.[5]

From a very early age, Ron showed his love of competition that would become one of his trademarks. When 11-year old Ronnie Norick began working at Bowlarena, his dad and granddad bowled in the men's league. So Ron became interested in bowling and actually became pretty good at it. He started bowling in several leagues, including the "Friday night Travelling League,"

which was the real "hot-shot" league of the day. It was a scratch league, where only the best bowlers would participate. There were about 16 teams in the league, and every Friday night they would go to a different bowling alley.

When Ron was in high school, he and his buddy Mac Matthews would go to nearby towns like Kingfisher, El Reno, and Pauls Valley and challenge the house. These two guys were real-life hustlers. They would go in and bowl two games for $5 a game and then $5 for highest pin total for the two games, meaning that there was $15 total at stake. Ron and Mac figured it took them about 30 minutes to bowl those two games and earn that $15. Not bad money for a short night's work.

At the age of 16, Ron decided he would turn his talent at bowling into some real money, so he entered the City Tournament. He won $1,200 in that tournament, which was pretty big money for an Oklahoma City teenager in 1957.[6]

Ron also had started playing golf at about age 10 or 11, and in fact, the legendary U.C. Ferguson, from Lincoln Park Golf Course, built Ron's first club. Jim Norick had taken a ladies' 3 wood to Ferguson who cut it down to a size that Ron could play with. So Ron started going out and playing golf with his dad at Lincoln after work, and Ferguson would always take time to work with young Ron. He and Ron became life long friends and when Ron was elected mayor in 1987, Ferguson was Ron's eyes and ears for Oklahoma City's public golf courses.

Jim Norick was an original member at the old Hillcrest Golf & Country Club, now Willow Creek Golf & Country Club, in south Oklahoma City. When Ron was 13 and not at work, Jim would take him to Hillcrest and drop him off on his way to

Norick Brothers. Ron would play golf, putt, and hit golf balls all day.

When Ron was a sophomore at Northwest Classen High School, he went out for the golf team. The school golf team had a young golfer named Chris Kauffman who would become a life-long friend and playing partner with Ron. They often played at the old Meridian Golf Course, located on the northwest corner of Northwest 23rd Street and Meridian Avenue.

Ron played baseball from grade school at Hawthorne Elementary through 'Y' ball in junior high at Taft all the way into high school at Northwest Classen. He was a left-handed pitcher, and in the early 1950s, not too many southpaws were pitching in little league baseball. Ron always believed that this gave him an advantage, because the kids he faced had not experienced too many pitches from that side of pitcher's mound. While at Hawthorne, pitching his three-inning stint, the limit you could pitch back then, Ron struck out all nine men he faced. He stayed with it and played baseball until his sophomore year at Northwest Classen.

In 1957, Ron, went out for the school golf team. But suddenly something happened to Ron that only Jim Thorpe would understand. The Oklahoma Secondary Schools Activities Association (OSSAA), the ruling body of high school sports, found out that young Ron Norick had won money bowling in various city and state tournaments.

The OSSAA declared him a professional athlete ineligible for high school athletic competition. The group told Ron that if he would tell them he was sorry and ask for their forgiveness, they would reconsider his eligibility. Ron told them he had not done anything wrong, that he did not take money from any organized team to play for them, and would not apologize. So he was barred from competing in high school sports.[7]

Ron continued bowling and was so good at it that he started considering turning pro in the sport. He continued bowling and playing softball until after college graduation when he blew out a knee playing in a Norick Brothers' company softball game. He continued playing golf and would continue to play the rest of his life, becoming a scratch golfer. In fact, he and his buddy Chris Kauffman would win several championships together. However, his bowling days were over.

This pattern of competitiveness which began in grade school at Hawthorne Elementary continued to be a part of everything Ron Norick attempted to do, including being mayor of the 28th largest city in the United States and competing with cities twice Oklahoma City's size to land major economic projects. He was not afraid to take on the house and would not back down if he thought he was right.[8]

Most good political science books tell you that one of the most valuable traits a politician can have is to be an entrepreneur. The ability to sell one's self and one's ideas, as well as the ability to make something work, is vital to achieving success. Ron Norick always had that quality, and it made him quite successful.

In 1973, Ron's grandfather, Henry Norick, who was chairman of the board of Norick Brothers, died. Ron's father, Jim, became chairman of the board and president, and Ron's grandmother, Ruth Norick, became chairman emeritus. Ron continued as vice president of manufacturing.

In the early 1970's, when computer systems for car dealers were still in their infancy, Norick Brothers was selected by General Motors as one of the pilot companies with IBM, Reynolds & Reynolds, ADP, and Singer to develop a communication system between the Detroit manufacturing facilities and car dealerships. The idea was to help the dealers order parts and transmit warranty documents electronically, thus allowing quick response

Left to right: J.R. McConnell, Ron, Henry, and Jim Norick, and Jerry Roll from the Norick Brothers Printing Company. The Noricks had built the company into a worldwide printing business operated out of Oklahoma City. *Courtesy Ron Norick.*

time. Prior to this, dealers would fill out a warranty form, mail it to Detroit, and if it had a mistake on it, Detroit would then send it back to the dealer and it would start all over. In the meantime, the dealer would not get paid until it was approved, so a lot of money was floating around in limbo. This new electronic transaction would cut the waiting period from weeks to hours. Ron Norick and Norick Brothers, along with some pretty big players, helped develop that program. However, the further along Ron went with the program, the more he realized that they were in over their heads. Ron knew that it would take millions of research dollars before they would ever realize a profit, and he knew that they could not play that game. He wanted to strictly be in the forms end of the business. Norick Brothers did not have the capital, or the means to raise it, without going public. They did not want to go public because they were a family business and wanted to stay that way. Part of being an entrepreneur is knowing what you can do well and what you cannot. Understanding that, they sold this electronic part of the business to ADP.[9]

Norick Brothers bought land and began building at Southwest 15th Street and Council Road. This was going to be their manufacturing and stock forms warehouse where their customers could order off the shelf. Ron designed a new manufacturing facility and had preliminary architectural plans drawn because they were beginning to bust at the seams in their present location. But on February 19, 1975, a three-alarm fire at Norick Brothers almost burned the entire manufacturing plant down. The fire penetrated the press room where there were nine big rotary presses, the heart of the business. Three of those had to be sent back to the manufacturer to be repaired and the rest were rebuilt on the floor. So Ron's thinking about one large manufacturing plant changed after the fire. For several weeks after the fire, Ron was at the building day and night, shifting orders from Oklahoma

City to outside suppliers and physically rebuilding the facility. It was during this time that he decided they should not put all their eggs into one basket, and that building just one big plant did not make any sense. As a result, the 15th Street project was scrapped.[10]

Norick Brothers had warehouse space and offices in San Francisco and Los Angeles, California, and Chicago, Illinois, and, after the fire, needed to divide their manufacturing. So in 1976 they began looking for additional manufacturing locations. Ron had looked in several states and had narrowed his search to right-to-work states. He went to Kings Mountain, North Carolina, where he found an old abandoned furniture manufacturer. The building had only been used about three or four years when the company closed. The Kings Mountain Industrial Authority, in this town of about 8,000 people, who along with the bank, had put up the bonds to build the facility. They were literally sinking with the debt of the empty building. Ron bought the 40,000 square-foot building for $300,000. The Kings Mountain plant was equipped and opened in 1977. Then in 1982, a West Coast manufacturing plant was established in North Las Vegas, Nevada. Norick Brothers was now well situated on both coasts and in the middle of the country. By this time, Norick Brothers employed more than 400 people.[11]

In December, 1976, Norick Brothers was a union shop with two unions – the printers' union, which would include all the printing press operators, and the bindery union. It was negotiation time for the printers' union and Ron Norick, as vice president of manufacturing, would handle the negotiations. The local union was represented by the International Pressman's Union with a union representative from Atlanta, Georgia. The union representative came to Oklahoma City during the negotiations and talked the local union into going on strike against Norick

Brothers. On December 19, 1976, the members of the printers' union went on strike. Ron could not understand why his employees would be walking a picket line instead of working just six days before Christmas.

It is interesting here to note that Norick Brothers, along with the Oklahoma Publishing Company, had faced a strike once before in the 1950s. The typesetters union struck against both firms. The two families, Norick and Gaylord, helped each other during that strike, stuck together, and broke the union. Ron has always believed that this is where the close family ties between the Noricks and Gaylords emerged.[12]

When the union went out on strike at Norick Brothers in December of 1976, management started running the printing presses. Ron would come to work with the management and non-union employees in the morning and would walk through the picket line. Since Ron had always been good to the employees and had a good relationship with them, he was able to cross the line without problems. In fact, Ron had grown up with most of the people on the picket line and they were beginning to feel a little awkward knowing they were on the wrong side of this strike. By the weekend, it was very cold outside and the union representative from Atlanta who talked them into going out on strike got on an airplane and went home for Christmas. The employees were left marching in the bitter Oklahoma cold. That was when Ron knew things would change.

Ron received a call from the local union officials asking for a meeting at the official's house that evening. They told Ron that they had made a mistake and wanted to know what he would offer them to end the strike. Ron told them he would honor the last offer he had proposed, but no union security clause. He told them that if they came back, there would be no union. They agreed, and Ron told them that starting Saturday morning, they would be interviewing people for the jobs at the plant. If they came down, they could apply for their jobs on a first-come, first-serve basis. They agreed to the terms, and all the employees except four or five local organizers showed up and received their jobs. They were happy and the Norick family was happy to have them back at work. Norick Brothers took care of their employees, provided them good retirement plans, rotated their jobs, offered them plenty of overtime, and cared about them as people. Norick Brothers was a family business and treated its employees like family. It was a bad strike for a bad reason, but ended on a positive note. The following spring, 1977, the bindery union contract was open for negotiation. They never had a negotiating session and the union went away. They knew that the only contract Ron would sign would be the same one, with the union security clause withdrawn. Norick Brothers had become an open shop.[13]

In 1978, Ron joined with a group of investors to return ice hockey to Oklahoma City after the original Oklahoma City Blazers had suspended operations. Ron was managing general partner and general manager of the Oklahoma City Stars from 1978 to 1980. The Stars were associated with the Minnesota North Stars of the National Hockey League. The investors eventually sold the team in 1980 to businessman John Hail who maintained the team until it folded in 1982.

In 1980, at the age of 39, Ron became president of Norick Brothers and led the company until 1992, when the family decided it was time to sell to Reynolds & Reynolds, their life-long competitors. Since those days, Ron has worked with his family business, Norick Investments, his son's racing team, his advertising agency, and his real estate development firm. Always an entrepreneur, Ron Norick continues to be successful.

CHAPTER XII

RON NORICK
THE POLITITIAN

RON DID NOT REMEMBER A LOT ABOUT HIS DAD'S FIRST RACE for the City Council in 1951. Ron was 10 years old at the time, but when Jim ran for mayor in 1959 things were a little different. Ron was a senior in high school and he and about a dozen of his classmates put out yard signs and handed out flyers. In fact, they would ride an old retired fire truck around with signs on the side saying "Norick for Mayor." When they would spot a group of people, they would stop and hand out flyers.

It was the old style political campaign, complete with walking, shaking hands, and holding political rallies. It was a fun, door-to-door, corner-to-corner, press-the-flesh type of campaign, and the high school kids loved it.

When the recount was called for after Jim's third place finish in the close primary, Jim and his campaign staff were concerned about the security of the ballot boxes. So Jim assigned people to take shifts watching the county court house vault which contained the ballot boxes to

Ron announces his intention to run for mayor. Ron would soon become the first son of a mayor to be elected mayor. *Courtesy Ron Norick.*

make sure they were not tampered with. Young Ron Norick was assigned to sit by the vault and guard the ballot boxes on the night shift. He sat at the County Election Board all night long with his chair leaning up against the vault.[1]

The next morning, the workers came in wanting to get into the vault, and Ron stood his ground and would not let them in. A photographer with *The Daily Oklahoman* even came down and took a picture of Ron refusing to let the sheriff into the vault. Ron immediately called his Dad, who told him not to let them in and that his attorneys would be there shortly. Ron told the sheriff that his Dad had told him not to leave that vault, and he was not going to move from that spot.

Jim and his attorney arrived, and they ended up holding the recount in the vault. They would take the ballots out of the box one at a time, inspect the ballot while the judge, the attorneys for both sides, and young Ron Norick watched. If someone wanted to contest a ballot for any reason, the judge would rule right then as to who would receive the vote or whether the ballot would be voided. After the recount, Jim Norick was declared the second place candidate over Merton Bulla by a single vote. As history notes, Jim went on to be elected mayor of Oklahoma City following the runoff election against Charles Burba.[2]

After high school, Ron attended the University of Oklahoma for a period of time before deciding he did not like OU because it was just too big. After meeting with Dean Willis Wheat, Ron enrolled at Oklahoma City University and majored in business management. He liked the smaller class size, 20-30 instead of 200, made good grades, and eventually made the President's Honor Roll. During his senior year at OCU in 1963, Ron's dad was running for re-election as mayor. The ARG had put together their slate of candidates to run against the four incumbent city council members and mayor. This group was basically, accord-

ing to Ron, the elitists of that time, and they wanted to take over City Hall with their candidates.[3]

The ARG supported candidate to run against Jim Norick for mayor was Jack Wilkes, the president of OCU. This obvi-

The Noricks, Ron and Jim, at the Norick Brothers plant. By 1986, things were going well enough at the plant that Ron did not need to spend all of his time there overseeing the business. There was time to think about civic responsibilities like running for office. *Courtesy Ron Norick.*

ously was very awkward for Ron, since he was now a senior at the university, and well known in the business school. The faculty of the business school was supporting Jim Norick, and did not think Wilkes should be in politics. The Bishop of the Methodist Church at the time, also tried to talk Wilkes out of running.[4]

When Wilkes ended up winning the race, as did the other four ARG candidates, Ron was devastated. Coming back to class at OCU the day after the election was a very hard thing for young Ron Norick to do. He went on to receive his degree from

OCU in business management and began his career at Norick Brothers. For 22 years he had been content to spend his time at the family business and avoid politics. Then in October of 1986, several people came to see Ron about running for a seat on the Oklahoma City Council, Ward 8. At the time, everything was going well at Norick Brothers, and Ron did not need to be at the plant 10 hours a day. Ron had time on his hands, and the idea interested him.

Rumors were beginning to circulate that current mayor, Andy Coats, might not run for re-election. Ron figured that as long as he was thinking about running for office, he should think about running for the highest available office. He had never been one who liked being second. In all the civic clubs and organizations he had belonged to, Ron had always ended up being elected president. He felt that if he was going to serve in an organization he wanted to go as high as he could go as an office holder.

Ron tried calling Mayor Coats several times to find out if he was running for re-election and never received a return phone call. Ron even called the mayor's secretary, Fran Cory, several times asking for Mayor Coats to call him. Finally, Ron decided that regardless of what the mayor was going to do, he was going to run for mayor. By this time, January of 1987, Ward 4 City Councilman Pete White had announced his intention to run for mayor.[5]

One morning about 7:00 a.m., Ron called his Dad and told him he wanted to come over and talk to him and his Mom. When he arrived, he poured a cup of coffee, looked at his parents and told them he wanted to run for mayor. Jim asked, "Why in the world would you want to do that?" Ron answered that he really wanted to do it and saw that both his Mom and Dad were in shock. They told him if that was what he wanted to do, they would help him in any way they could. Just like Henry Norick had given his son, Jim, his full support in 1959, Ron received Jim and Madalynne's full blessings as they stood behind him in his quest for mayor.

There was good news and bad news about the timing of his decision. The good news was that by waiting until January to make his decision, there was only one month before filing in February and two months before the election in March so it would be a short campaign. The bad news was that by waiting until January to make his decision, he only had one month before filing in February and only two months before the election in March so it would be a short campaign!

Ron set up his campaign office on the corner of Northwest 24th Street and Classen Boulevard and began

Ron announces his intention to run for mayor as his father, Jim, looks on. Jim, the first Oklahoma City-born mayor was there to cheer his son on to become the first son of a mayor to be elected mayor. *Courtesy Ron Norick.*

a telephone campaign. Long time friend Bill Johnstone was his campaign manager. Johnstone, head of City Bank and Trust, told Ron he did not know anything about running a campaign. "I don't know anything about running for mayor, either," Ron told him, "so we'll do it together." There was a blizzard that January that shut down just about all traffic in the city. Using the telephone, Ron and Bill were able to catch a lot of people at home and get them to be hosts at his first fundraiser.[6]

Ron's campaign team was composed of his mom & dad, Bill Johnstone, Allen Coles, Harold Hite, Glenda Phillips, Bill Bishop, Jim Scott, and Jack Cornett. They raised about $130,000 and spent every penny of it, including $10,000 of Ron's money.[7]

There were seven candidates, but clearly the biggest threat was from Ward 4 City Councilman and southside attorney Pete White. Ron and Pete had several debates during the campaign, with each one carrying their own message. Ron's was "Norick Means

Business," meaning he wanted to run the City like a business. In his campaign advertisements, Ron said, "As a businessman, not a politician, I can offer a new perspective to many of the issues we face." For the last six weeks of the campaign, Ron went door-to-door every weekend using a precinct list that showed who voted in the last election. Using the list, he hit the heavy precincts in wards 1, 5 and 8. It was a close election all the way, with all the polls pretty even until the last few days of the campaign. That was when they started showing the "Norick Means Business" message was starting to make gains.

Ron visits with citizens after a public forum. Jim has his back to the camera watching his son pursue the office Jim held 16 years earlier. *Courtesy Ron Norick.*

Appearing at a public forum with five other candidates, Ron had several questions for city councilman White. White held a seat on the city's water trust and Ron questioned some of the business decisions of the trust.

"I want to know why $120,000 was paid to the municipal counselor," Ron began, "who is already on the payroll of Oklahoma City, for fees? I want to know why $15,000 was spent on top of that for furniture for the municipal counselor's office?" Ron said that if the city attorney needed furniture that he should have submitted a request through normal budgeting channels. White responded, "If you want to talk about the water trust, I can. But I'm tired of cheap shots."

The headline of the next day's story in the paper read, "2 Mayorial Candidates Skirmish." *The Daily Oklahoman* described the two men as "far apart politically and philosophically as they

ABOVE: At Ron's first watch party, the family gathered to show their support. Standing left to right are Ron's aunts, Marjorie Norick, Frances Norick Lilly and his father, Jim. Seated is Ron's grandmother, Ruth. *Courtesy Ron Norick.*

LEFT: Ron and his grandmother, Ruth, are seen celebrating at his first watch party at Northwest 24th Street and Classen Boulevard. She lived to see her son and grandson serve the Oklahoma City community as mayor, the only father-son pair to serve as mayors in the history of the City. *Courtesy Ron Norick.*

Mayoral candidate Ron Norick waits for results in the election of 1987 along with then-City Manager Terry Childers. It was a short evening as Ron knew the results just a couple of hours after the polls closed. *Courtesy Ron Norick.*

are geographically." White was a southside Democrat and Ron was a northside Republican. In an editorial, the newspaper wrote, "...one candidate stands out, far above the pack. Ron Norick clearly is the best choice for mayor."

On election night, the Norick watch party set up at the campaign headquarters on Northwest 24th Street & Classen Boulevard, right across from the old milk bottle building. It was a relatively small area, so 50 people in the room would have looked good. There were probably 100 people there that night, and they were anticipating a runoff between Norick and White. But as the evening proceeded, the crowd started buzzing with the possibility that Ron might just win the election without a runoff. Harold Hite, political analyst in the Norick campaign, told Ron an hour and a half before the results started coming in that he would win without a runoff. Sure enough, about 10:00 p.m., the press started flocking in to get Norick's reaction to the fact he was going to be the next mayor of Oklahoma City.

Pete White called Norick about 2:30 a.m., to concede the election and congratulated Norick on his campaign. He was very gracious and, in fact, since that time became a good friend of Norick's, remaining very complimentary of the things Ron did in office. White even went so far as to once tell Norick that "he had been a lot better mayor than he [White] could have ever been."[8]

In the field of seven candidates, Ron Norick received 50.1% of the vote and was elected without a runoff. Ron would go on to win his next two re-election campaigns by 70 percent or more. He was sworn into office on April 14, 1987, by his father, Mayor Jim Norick.

CHAPTER XIII

RON'S FIRST TERM

THREE NEW FACES AT CITY HALL were to be sworn in on April 14, 1987. These three - Mark Schwartz, Beverly Hodges, and Ronald J. Norick - would change the direction of Oklahoma City.

A familiar face, and a proud father, performed the swearing in ceremony for Ron. Jim Norick asked Ron to raise his right hand and repeat the vows for the office of mayor. It was a milestone for Oklahoma City. It was the first time a son of a former mayor also became mayor.

Wasting no time, Ron abolished all nine standing city council committees and various ad hoc committees. "I did that because I wanted to take a fresh look at the make-up of the council," Ron told a business group luncheon. He said the committees "were probably set up a number of years ago and probably were out of tune with what this city needs at this time."[1]

He also wanted to improve the bidding, procurement, and payment

The weight of the office sometimes made being mayor a lonely job. Ron Norick knew that he could never give up on bringing business to Oklahoma City, because that's what he knew best. One of the early plums he went after was an American Airlines maintenance and engineering center. *Courtesy Ron Norick.*

procedures for contractors and vendors doing business with the city. Describing the old process as cumbersome, Ron added, "As a businessman, I like to be paid within 30 days after doing work, so should these businessmen and women."[2]

After two weeks on the job, Ron felt more comfortable than he originally thought. Based on his father's experience, he knew it was more of a job than just a figurehead. "There are tremendous demands on your time," Ron told a reporter. "A lot of it has to do with the fact I'm new and people want to meet the new mayor."[3] Feeling that comments from the citizens of Oklahoma City would make him a stronger mayor, Ron liked to say hello to people so that they felt comfortable in walking up and saying something to him.

New Mayor Ron Norick raises his right hand to take the oath of office from former mayor and father, Jim Norick on April 13, 1987. It was the first time the son of a former mayor of Oklahoma City was sworn in. *Courtesy The Daily Oklahoman.*

An early water project popped up for Ron when in May the opportunity presented itself to pay off McGee Creek Reservoir and save $211 million. A 50-year payment plan with the federal government was to cost Oklahoma City a total of $367 million. If Oklahoma City payed the government $69.9 million now, they would save the $211 million. As a result of President Ronald Reagan's push to make smaller government, the feds were offering this deal. The city manager, Terry Childers, supported the buyout and so did Ron.

The state's economic conditions had caused some belt tightening all over. A Daily Oklahoman editorial commented on how Ron and the city had dealt with the budget problems by saying, "Oklahoma taxpayers would have been much better off if Governor Henry Bellmon and the legislature had demonstrated the courage and fiscal responsibility displayed by Oklahoma City Mayor Ron Norick and the Oklahoma City Council." Referring to the raising of state taxes instead of the city cutting down to stay within budget, the editorial went on to say, "Oklahoma City officials could give state government officials some lessons in belt tightening."[4]

In late July that first year of Ron's term, he was invited to the White House to get a firsthand description of President Reagan's proposed "Economic Bill of Rights." This represented Reagan's desire to privatize as much of the federal government's operation as possible. With a Democratic Congress, the chance of passage was slim. Even though he supported certain parts of the package as a private citizen, Ron could not support it as mayor.

In September, Ron dealt with a deteriorating Myriad Convention Center. A report told of loss of convention business due to a leaky roof, cracks in the floor, and lack of state-of-the-art facilities. The need for better hotel facilities added to the problem and established one part of what would justify a future MAPS program.

Toward the end of 1987, Ron joined with Tulsa mayor, Dick Crawford, to ask Governor Bellmon to support legislation to help the cities with obligation bonds and how they are voted on. Ron would work with Tulsa more in the future.

Ron started the new year of 1988 with a program called "Adopt-A-Pothole." With a lot less money than needed to patch potholes, the program provided for a $10 donation by an individual to get a pothole filled. "If we can sell 3,000 potholes, that's $30,000 that doesn't have to come out of the budget," Ron told a reporter.

The story went out on Associated Press and two Louisiana radio disc jockeys read about it and adopted a pothole. It became a national story and money started coming in from all over the United States. *The Wall Street Journal* even reported the story.

Ron remembers that on this occasion, he learned his first political lesson. When he announced this "Adopt-A-Pothole" program at a press conference, he was criticized by some council members because he had not informed them prior to the announcement. He realized that whether they thought it was a good thing or a bad thing he was promoting, council members needed to know ahead of time. They might want to join in or they might not, but they deserved the option. One thing they did not want was to be caught not knowing.

On March 2, 1988, Penn Square Mall reopened as a reinvented shopping center. Mayor Ron Norick spoke in the new courtyard saying, "Oklahoma is alive and well!" In talking about the mall owners and developers, he said, "You don't come into a city unless you feel a real future in Oklahoma City."

Ron Norick and attorney John Williams at a McGee Creek Authority meeting in Southeastern Oklahoma. As chairman and a trustee of the authority, Norick regularly attended meetings concerning this important water resource. *Courtesy Oklahoma City Water Utilities Trust.*

An even bigger grand opening came on March 25 when the Crystal Bridge was dedicated. The 220 foot long, three-story garden was officially opened when Ron cut the ribbon at 11:00 a.m.

Ron's first year as mayor ended with a stint with the Oklahoma City Fire Department at Station #5, Northwest 23rd Street and Broadway. "My main purpose in spending time here," Ron said, "was to get a better understanding of what these guys do. I grew up in my business in the plant. If you want to know what's going on, you have to get in the trenches. Next time they talk about needing additional equipment or manpower, I will be able to see where they're headed. Seeing what they do firsthand is different than just hearing about it."[5]

Ron remembered trying to get some sleep, but then the alarm went off, the lights went on and it "jolted me out of bed." He rushed to the pole and slid down, only to see everyone waiting on him. He rode with the squad that went to all of the wrecks and shootings, so he made several runs on his watch.

The breakfasts were the biggest he had ever seen. There was chili, eggs, and cheese. Ron also would see the captains drop by the station "just to visit," but really to see how things were going.

That was the beginning of a strong working relationship between Ron and the Fire Department. At Christmas time, it became a tradition for Ron to make a special homemade

Ron established a great working relationship with the city offices, and the Oklahoma City Fire Department was one of the best. At Christmas, he began a tradition of delivering homemade spiced tea to each of the fire stations. *Courtesy Ron Norick.*

spiced tea. He would be accompanied by Chief Gary Marrs or Assistant Chief Jon Hansen to each of the fire stations carrying these quart jars of tea. Starting the deliveries at 6:00 p.m., it would be midnight before he finished.

Ron Norick tried to bridge the gap between Tulsa and Oklahoma City at the start of his administration. Joining with Tulsa Mayor Roger Randle in September of 1988, the two mayors and their wives dined with businessmen and city officials first in Tulsa, then in Oklahoma City.

Ron and Carolyn hosted Roger and Judy Randle at Remington Park. Among those in attendance were most of the city council

To Rich — who has become A[...]
life. Thanks for being such a goo[...]

Jeric[...]

el a part of my
end —

Edwards

members, Ray and Lou Ackerman, Jay and Pat Edwards, Dan Hogan, Stanley and Suzie Hupfeld, Clyde Ingle, Bill and Ann Johnstone, John and Eleanor Kirkpatrick, Stan and Marcia Lybarger, Dusty Martin, Ed and Judy Miller, and David and Sharon Vance. It was the beginning of several joint functions between Oklahoma's largest metropolitan areas.[6]

The Mayor's Christmas Party was something that Ron looked forward to each year. It was held in the Civic Center Music Hall or the Myriad Convention Center and city buses provided free transportation. The tradition was something that he cherished in terms of gift giving to the children of Oklahoma City and

Ron Norick visits with Congressman Mickey Edwards in his Washington, D.C. office in 1989, along with Councilwoman Jackie Carey, Mayor's Assistant Rick Moore, and Councilman Dan Fine. They were discussing Oklahoma City's legislative issues for the coming year. Moore had been on Edwards' staff and helped strengthen the ties for the city to Washington. *Courtesy Rick Moore.*

included his Dad playing Christmas songs with his band. It was a chance for smiles on children's faces when they did not have much to smile about. It gave people the opportunity to see what the season was truly about and how one could count their blessings.

On December 9, 1988, the mayor's office announced Ron's choice for his new assistant, Rick Moore. *The Daily Oklahoman* reported that, "Moore, 36, has worked for the past several years as a staff assistant for U.S. Congressman Mickey Edwards and has been involved with economic development and foreign government relations." Norick added, "Aside from Rick Moore's commitment to Oklahoma City, he will also help strengthen the city's ties in Washington, D.C." Mike McAuliffe, who previously held the position, was named chief of staff for the mayor and council.[7]

The new year of 1989 started with a disagreement between Ron and City Manager Terry Childers. With an upcoming vote on a penny sales tax increase, Childers held a press conference the Thursday before the vote without conferring with the mayor.

Childers warned of dire consequences if the tax, to be used for the fire and police departments, was not passed. He said there would be layoffs. He also told the press that if it did pass, the first $5 million would be needed just to maintain current levels.

An upset Ron Norick flatly responded, "He's wrong on that. Why he decided to have that press conference on Thursday, I do not know." Ron had told residents at Town Hall meetings that all of the money would go toward hiring additional police officers and firefighters as well as the construction of five new fire stations.

As for possible layoffs if the vote failed, Ron said, "It's just not going to happen. There are too many other areas we can cut before we get to police and fire." The effect on the election could be negative and Ron called it "unfortunate" that Childers would come out with these statements just before the vote.[8] On Tuesday, January 10, 1989, the tax was defeated.

An editorial in the January 12 *Daily Oklahoman* said, "it's time for Childers to leave." Norick responded that he's "not going to cry over spilt milk." It was the beginning of the end for Childers, however. The final straw came in June when Childers presented the budget. The mayor and four council members decided parts needed to be rewritten before approval and this did not set well with the city manager. Childers and Jack Cornett had battled over personnel. Cornett wanted an assistant city manager fired and suggested a replacement for him.

"If you are truly unhappy with the city manager," Childers told him, "make a change. Don't destroy the system in place to help your friends and buddies. Don't strip me of my ability to get my job done." When asked later if he planned to follow Cornett's suggestions, he replied, "Hell, no!"

Councilwoman Jackie Carey said she resented having to adjust the budget at the eleventh hour. This process went on all day and into the night. It was an extremely difficult day. Ron called it "one of the hardest days on the job I've ever had." Ron saw himself as a consensus builder and not a confrontational guy. "There wasn't much consensus building that day," Ron would later remember. The council's session lasted 14 hours that June Tuesday. Revenue was $12 million short of the city's needs and licensing fees and permits were increased. As the council hammered away at the changes, Childers moved things around to come up with the rest.[9]

Childers resigned in July to enter private business. He said he left for two reasons, his family and a desire to enter private business.

Business was what Ron Norick was all about. He was serious about bringing business to Oklahoma City. His first big brush with this goal came when Ed Stewart, spokesman for American Airlines, confirmed on March 20, 1989, that a site search was underway for a new maintenance and engineering center. "The center is expected to create 4,500 new jobs within its first five years of operation," Stewart said. "We would like it to be built as soon as possible. Our fleet is expanding so rapidly."[10]

Ron and a delegation flew to Dallas-Fort Worth with an inducement proposal for American. The proposed Oklahoma City site would be located along the east side of the east runway at Will Rogers World Airport.

After meeting with Oklahoma's Congressional delegation three days later in Washington, D.C., Robert Crandall, Chairman of American, said he was impressed by the support given the project by the Oklahoma City community and congressional delegation. Crandall said that Oklahoma City had "an excellent runway, good financing, good labor market and an airport trust." He also liked its close proximity to their main maintenance center in Tulsa.[11]

Councilman Jim Scott proclaimed, "We are very optimistic." Jimmy Lyles, Oklahoma City Chamber president said, "We don't enter anything that we don't think we can win." Ron Norick said, "We are definitely in the hunt." The chief competition was Fort Worth – American's headquarters.

On June 7, American announced its selection of Fort Worth, but added 1,600 jobs to its Tulsa facility benefiting Oklahoma with a $150 million investment. Ron said, "Obviously, we are very disappointed that it will not come to Oklahoma City, but I am extremely pleased that the State of Oklahoma will receive some benefit."

"This puts the world on notice that Oklahoma City is back in the industrial development business," Ed Martin, chairman of the Oklahoma City Chamber declared. When Governor Henry Bellmon asked Crandall if there was anything else Oklahoma City could have done, Crandall explained that DFW Airport was the deciding factor and Oklahoma City had done all that was

needed. The expansion at Tulsa was due to the "tireless efforts of Governor Bellmon and his associates" according to Robert W. Baker, American's senior vice president of operations.[12]

It was a good educational experience for Ron and the city. It was tough to get over, but this was a big year for Oklahoma City. One of the major dedications in town that year was I-235, the Centennial Expressway. It was named in honor of the city's 100th birthday. It stretched from I-40 on the south, ran north on the old Broadway Extension to I-44 between Northeast 50th and Northeast 63rd Streets. That same stretch was the north-south rail line where the Oklahoma City Station was located 100 years before in preparation for the Land Run of 1889. Ron called the new highway a modern monument to those who came before us. He added that it marked "our passage into the new century."[13]

The saving of the Skirvin Hotel became a mission for Ron that same year. It had changed hands three times in four years and finally went into foreclosure in 1987. It closed without notice for renovations on October 7, 1988. Savoy Hotels and Resorts was the current owner in April of 1989 when Ron threatened to withdraw the city's support for a $3.8 million loan to the company. They had failed to produce a letter of credit from a financial institution to complete the deal. On May 9, the council voted to cancel, again leaving the fate of the 78-year-old hotel up in the air.[14]

As 1989 progressed, a trend was developing in city council votes. The lines were usually drawn five to four. The majority was usually Ron, Mark Schwartz, Dan Fine, Jack Cornett, and Jim Scott. The minority was I.G. Purser, Beverly Hodges, Goree James, and Jackie Carey. Occasionally, Beverly Hodges and Mark Schwartz would switch positions and vote with the other group. However, one thing they supported unanimously was to have a special election on June 20 for a ¾ cent sales tax increase to benefit the police and fire departments. This was an effort to overcome the botched vote when Terry Childers called his press conference back in January.

Debbie Blackburn, director of the Neighborhood Alliance of Oklahoma City, presented a 40,000 signature petition to Ron for this vote to happen. It took the Council just two minutes to unanimously vote for its passage. Blackburn said it was a grass-roots neighborhood movement to get this tax help back in front of the voters. She said the city called the shots in the January 10 election that failed, but this one comes from the people.[15] This time, it passed.

The new year of 1990 saw Oklahoma City looking a decade ahead with a special conference attended by more than 2,000 women. The Mayor's Conference for Women in the 1990s was held March 30 and 31. Chaired by Terry Neese and Linda Richardson, the conference provided a forum for women to determine ways they could establish positive economic, social, and political programs. Ron noted that by the year 2000, 47 percent of the nation's workforce would be female.[16]

Ron continued his cooperative approach with Tulsa in a couple more areas which started with the Oklahoma Cup Run between the two cities to raise money for the public schools in both cities. Governor Bellmon said, "I hope this will be a more healthy rivalry than some of the things that have gone on between Oklahoma City and Tulsa."[17]

In March, 1990, the Oklahoma City AmCare ambulance service was combined with Tulsa's Emergency Medical Service Authority. AmCare was failing financially with Oklahoma City subsidizing it since November, 1989. Ron saw it as a good deal. "It should outlast all of us in office now. It's a really solid deal. Citizens should feel good about it," he told a reporter.[18]

At the same time, another airline deal was in the mix. Ron announced on March 26 that Oklahoma City had made the first cut for a new United Airlines repair facility. It would be the beginning of the biggest change ever for this 100-year-old city.

CHAPTER XIV

THE BIRTH OF MAPS:
The Rebirth of a City

RON NORICK NEVER THOUGHT HE WAS GOING TO RUN for more than one term as mayor. He remembered a statement made by Ward 8 Councilwoman Jackie Carey that had a huge impact on his time in office. Jackie and Ron had never really seen eye-to-eye on things, to a great extent because she wanted to run for mayor herself. There was one occasion about half way through his first term in office, when Jackie said, "Ron, for this city's sake you need to decide what you're going to do, and do it!"[1]

That was really good advice, and from that point on he remembered that admonition and really began to focus. Instead of just being a caretaker, he started focusing on issues that he wanted to work on to move this city forward.

One issue at the top of his list was the first long-term capital plan the city had ever had. The city was basically providing for its long-term

The official city portrait of Mayor Ronald J. Norick. *Courtesy Ron Norick.*

capital needs by taking whatever was left over at the end of the budget process and spending it on capital needs. As it turns out, there is never much left, so city-owned buildings, streets, and parks, were not being taken

care of. Ron knew that the city had to have a plan. He was in a business that required ordering equipment like new printing presses one or two years before they were needed. The presses were custom made and it took that long to build. Norick could have been without press capacity for a year or more if he had not had a plan in place for the future. He knew the city needed to do the same thing, plan for the future.

Infrastructure was a key issue. Bond issues for the infrastructure of Oklahoma City had not been passed since 1976, and that one was a small one. That meant that during the 1980s, because of the economic conditions of the time, Oklahoma City had not passed any bond issues to work on the infrastructure or any city-owned buildings. What that really meant was that Oklahoma City had gone 10 to12 years absorbing deterioration to streets, bridges, water lines, and sewer lines. Ron's first goal became helping the infrastructure.

Because Oklahoma City had not passed a bond issue in such a long time, city officials had to restore voter confidence. They did that by saying the city would not raise property taxes for the new bond issue, but rather would issue new debt only when the old bonds were retired. Norick told citizens that if their homes had gone without repairs and maintenance for 10 to12 years, think of the problems they would have. The voters knew he had a business background, and that he knew what he was talking about. That was where his business experience kicked in and really

made a difference. It was not a political issue, he told them, but a business issue. If you want the city to continue to deteriorate, do nothing. Norick told voters that if they waited until they could not drive on their streets to fix them, it would be too late; if they waited until the water system went out, it would be too late. He wanted the city to fix these things while people could still drive on the streets, still have water every morning, and stay ahead of the game. Norick also specified the projects and their costs, as mandated by law, and set about to convince the voters. The people went along with that, and passed the 1989 bond

LET'S GET UNITED!
10,000
Permanent Jobs

United Airlines is nearly ready to begin construction of a Billion Dollar Maintenance Center which will create at least 10,000 new and permanent jobs. That doesn't count the 13,000 construction-related jobs that will be created when construction is at its peak.

The United facility is the biggest economic development project in the nation and ninety metropolitan areas have been competing for it. Now only nine competitors remain and Oklahoma County is a leader among those nine.

★ The economic impact of the project is enormous. It will pump $700 Million a year into the economy of Central Oklahoma.

★ United is waiting to announce where it will locate the huge maintenance center until after Oklahoma County votes on a temporary one-cent sales tax which would go to fund a small portion of the project.

★ The temporary tax is absolutely limited to no more than 33 months and absolutely earmarked for construction of the project.

★ The temporary tax will not go into effect unless and until United Airlines signs a contract to locate the facility in Oklahoma County.

Let's show United Airlines we want those 10,000 jobs.

LET'S GET UNITED!
VOTE YES
TUESDAY, FEBRUARY 26

Paid for by Oklahomans United for Jobs
John Kilpatrick, Chairman
P.O. Box 368 ● Oklahoma City, OK 73101

issue, which at that time was the largest bond issue in Oklahoma City history.

Oklahoma City officials earned the voter confidence they needed. The city spent the money properly, the way they had told the voters they would, and for the projects they had promised. This would eventually be the confidence that helped pass the public safety sales tax in 1989, the 1991 sales tax for the Zoo, MAPS in 1993, the 1995 bond issue, the 2000 bond issue, the MAPS for Kids, and every other ballot put before the Oklahoma City voters. Some of Norick's Democrat friends in the Oklahoma legislature would tease him about being the "taxingest Republican" they had ever seen. That may be true, because even though he was a fairly conservative Republican on most issues, he was a real moderate when it came to social and fiscal issues. He had found that to get things done, you better not be either too extreme to the right or to the left, but be willing to work for the good of everyone. That was usually somewhere in the middle. That was the reason Ron Norick was so successful at the Capitol and City Hall, because he could usually find a middle ground somewhere. He could get along with both sides of the aisle.

During this time the city was experiencing a lot of success at the ballot box, but they were failing at another level of bringing in big economic development plums. Norick thought that by luring these high-paying, high-tech jobs to Oklahoma City, they could expand the tax base and prosper. American Airlines and United Airlines were probably the two largest opportunities at the time, but Oklahoma City landed neither of them. Ron did learn a lot from going through the process, such as what it takes to even be considered. Oklahoma City was finally getting on the map at a lot of levels. Oklahoma City was becoming known as a city trying to do something. The city had the resources and the people it took to make things work, but was continually being the bridesmaid. It always seemed to point back to the fact that the decision makers in the businesses Oklahoma City was trying to attract did not want to come here to live. Their perception of Oklahoma City was either negative or none. In fact, city officials would ask some of these people what they knew about Oklahoma City and they would either give a blank look or say something like, "Yeah, I saw the play or the movie," or "I have heard of Barry Switzer or Oklahoma football," or "the oil bust, or Penn Square Bank failure," or "the dust bowl." There was never anything really exciting coming out of their mouths.

But it was the United Airlines maintenance facility project that finally got Norick to do something about this neutral or negative image of Oklahoma City. The United Airlines maintenance facility project would be a gigantic economic boost to the city that won it. It would be 5,000 jobs, with salaries in the $40,000 plus yearly range. It would also bring in lots of satellite support business in the adjacent vicinity. More than 75 cities initially tried for this project.[2]

By January of 1991, Oklahoma City had become a top contender to land this plum project. Ed Bee, director of economic development for the Oklahoma City Chamber of Commerce said, "We probably won't have another opportunity like this for 10 years."[3]

Norick had announced on January 8 that he intended to run for re-election. But re-election would take a back seat to winning the United deal. At the same time he made the announcement, he was meeting with David Walters,

Oklahoma City Mayor Ron Norick addresses the Oklahoma House of Representatives requesting state incentives to help bring United Airlines maintenance facility to Oklahoma City.
Courtesy of Ron Norick.

the Governor-elect. Walters went public with information that he would do what he could to help. "It became clear," Walters told the media on January 8, "that in order to compete we had to move and that we couldn't wait for the regular session."[4] When he was inaugurated on January 15, 1991, three hours later the new governor spoke to the special session of the Legislature. He challenged them to "recognize our opportunities and seize the day."[5]

Resolutions passed, among others, allowed a sales tax exemption on construction materials, and after it was built, a tax exemption on parts for the airplanes. Oklahoma County set February 19 for a one-cent sales tax election. Revenue bonds issued by the Oklahoma City Airport Trust would pay for three-fourths of the plant's construction. United would pay off the bonds through lease payments. The one-cent sales tax would provide $120 million over a 33 month span to help with the rest.

Merle McCollum, chairman of Citizens Opposed to Outrageous Politics filed to run against Norick for mayor. He was quoted as saying he was running to "stop this epidemic of tax, tax, tax." He called the one-cent tax to attract United as "one of the biggest scams in Oklahoma."[6]

In early February, United sent out consultants to evaluate the different cities in the running for the plant. They researched the schools, housing markets, climate, crime, and entertainment. That last entry about entertainment or quality of life for United employees would come back to haunt Norick. City Councilman Jim Scott said his feeling was that the main competitors were Dulles in Virginia, Denver, Cincinnati, and Indianapolis. "I don't believe any other city has given United the options we've offered them," Scott added.[7]

A support rally was held in front of the Myriad to approve the one-cent sales tax. Several hundred people showed up to support the tax on this day before the vote. On February 26, the tax was approved by 72% with a total of 66,180 for passage. Norick said it showed Oklahomans wanted quality jobs and were willing to sacrifice for them. "Three years at one-cent is a minor investment," he added.[8]

A billboard near the entrance of United's headquarters in Chicago displayed a message from Oklahoma. With the red, white and blue United logo were the words, "Come Fly the Friendly Skies of Oklahoma City." This play on words of the company slogan was another effort to boost Oklahoma City's chances.

Norick won his first re-election bid on March 19, 1991. It was the largest mayoral election margin in more than 30 years, winning 80.3 per cent of the vote. However, he still was totally absorbed in the United effort. Norick and Scott had spent about 2,000 hours each on the project, including 10 full weekends. They both had paid most of their expenses.

It all came crashing down in October when Indianapolis was the announced winner. Norick was disappointed, but "very proud" of Oklahoma's effort. United officials said that Oklahoma City's proposal was "by far the best prepared, well organized, the most professional, the most courteous, the most responsive."[9]

But Norick was devastated. He could not believe that with all that had been put together, they still were not chosen. United Chairman Stephen Wolf had made the decision. Ron finally came to understand that Wolf looked at the two cities and decided he would rather be in a city where they had revitalized their downtown, brought in professional sports; in other words, their quality of life had been a key factor. Oklahoma City was in the same position that Indianapolis had been in the 1970's, with no vitality and no positive outlook. The dif-

Mayor Ron Norick with City Councilman and Oklahoma City Airport Trust member, Jim Scott looking on, announces that United Airlines will not come to Oklahoma City. It would turn out to be a defining moment in Oklahoma City history. *Courtesy The Daily Oklahoman.*

ference was that they had done something about their city, and Oklahoma City had not. Ron thought that if the citizens were willing to tax themselves to look better to other people, they ought to be willing to tax themselves to make themselves feel better about themselves. Norick was tired of finishing second to other cities, because if they had finished second, they might as well have finished 77th.

It was really this loss of an economic plum that gave birth to the idea of MAPS. Little did Norick know then that the loss was the best thing that ever happened to Oklahoma City. If they had won United, not only would Oklahoma City have ended up with an empty facility and a bankrupt company like Indianapolis would have, but no MAPS program would have been initiated.

As Norick looked at the cities that had been winning the economic development projects over Oklahoma City, he noticed similar traits: revitalized downtowns and public facilities. He started taking inventory of Oklahoma City's downtown and public facilities, and found a downtown that had lost most of its vitality and retail, and was like a ghost town after 6:00 p.m. on the weekday evenings and weekends. As for public facilities, the newest one the city had was the Myriad Convention Center, 20 years old and beginning to deteriorate. As for a ballpark, All-Sports Stadium had been built in 1964 and no longer passed city codes, let alone the newly passed Americans with Disabilities Act of 1990 requirements. In fact, the commissioner of minor league baseball told Norick that unless cities with substandard stadiums did something to make them more attractive, accessible, and user-friendly for both the players and the fans, they would start pulling franchises from cities. Even the 89ers team owner Jeffrey Loria, New York art dealer and later, famous owner of the world champion Florida

Marlins, was bringing Norick his ideas for a new or renovated stadium. The performing arts facility, the Civic Center, was a WPA project with only one renovation since the 1930s and was not allowing a lot of big shows like "Phantom of the Opera" to even come to Oklahoma City. The fairgrounds was in desperate need of assistance to keep the many national horse shows from leaving and going to cities with better facilities. The downtown public library, built in 1954, was outdated and in bad shape. The North Canadian River, which separated north and south Oklahoma City geographically, used to flood Oklahoma City on a regular basis in the early days, had been changed by the Corps of Engineers so that it would not flood as easily. They did such a good job of stopping the flooding that there was so little water in the river, Oklahoma City had the distinction of the only river in America needing to be mowed twice a year. Ron could see that every time he would pick up potential economic development prospects at the airport and drive them around town, the first thing they saw was crossing a bridge over a dry river bed. Things needed to change.[10]

As many people had come to say, Oklahoma City was one of the most studied cities in America. All kinds of studies had been conducted on various aspects of the community, but the results were put on shelves and nobody had ever come up with a plan to make the results of those studies happen or the funding to do them --- until now.

In 1988, Norick appointed the Downtown Redevelopment Task Force, a 16-member group, to look at what would be needed for a rebirth of the Downtown area. The group was co-chaired by James Harlow, Jr., of Oklahoma Gas and Electric Company (OG&E) and Nancy Anthony of the Oklahoma City Community Foundation. Other members included Jim Clark of B.C. Clark Jewelers, Oklahoma County Commissioner Shirley Darrell-Daniels, Mark

Elgin of Globe Life, Fred Hall of Fred Jones Industries, Clyde Ingle of the Oklahoma City Chamber of Commerce, Bill Johnstone of City Bank, Attorney Tom King, James Tolbert III of First National Corporation, and council members Goree James, Pete White, Beverly Hodges, I.G. Purser, and Jackie Carey.

In October of 1988, the group went to San Antonio, Texas, to learn how they were able to turn their downtown into a $1 billion-a-year tourist attraction. They came home enthusiastic about putting together their own list of four or five goals and getting started.[11]

After the United Airlines loss in 1992, Norick organized a small group of civic leaders to talk about

City Manager Don Bown and Mayor Ron Norick listen to a citizen at City Council. Bown was a big player as City Manager in the MAPS project development. *Courtesy Ron Norick.*

THOMAS P. HURLEY
CITY CLERK

the situation and see what, if anything, could be done to change it. These early meetings of the original group were attended by Mayor Ron Norick, Oklahoma City City Manager Don Bown, Oklahoma County Treasurer Joe B. Barnes, Chairman of the Oklahoma County Commissioners, Buck Buchanan, Oklahoma City Chamber of Commerce Executive Jimmy Lyles, Oklahoma City Chamber of Commerce incoming Chairman Ken Townsend, current Chamber Chairman Frank McPherson, Second Century & Urban Renewal member Bill Johnstone, Clayton I. Bennett, an at-large member, and, to staff the group, assistant to the mayor Rick Moore. Norick wanted the group to look at the discovery he had made and brainstorm as to how to fix it. The first organizational meetings were private meetings, behind closed doors. Norick felt that these early meetings should not be public, because it would stymie good discussion by just letting a reporter in the room. If there was a good brainstorming session going on, the ability to be creative and to be able to say whatever came to mind without worrying about how it sounded were necessary. The environment to throw a lot of things out, knowing that some of them would not make sense or be a good idea, was essential. If those early meetings of the origins of MAPS had been public meetings, MAPS might never have happened. Decisions about public business were not being made, but rather ideas were trying to be born which would lead to public business, and that would very definitely be carried out in the light of day.[12]

Don Bown, city manager from 1991 to 1998, remembers those early meetings.

"We developed a pattern of meeting once a week, prior to council meeting, to go over the council agenda. I would meet him (Ron) out at Norick Brothers, and we would go through the agenda and then we would have a period of time to talk about various other things in

the city, other than the agenda of the city council meetings. In those meetings, a lot of things were discussed,
and at the very beginning of these meetings, many of the
things talked about were plans that the city had money
for...such as the river study, the question about a ballpark,
the question of what were we going to do about the civic
center, the question about whether we should remodel
the Myriad Convention Center or should we build a new
arena. These were the kind of things Ron Norick was
talking about. And when it was finished, it became pretty
obvious from his view point that a lot of the planning for
a lot of the things we were talking about for the community, were studies that were already either underway or had
been completed in some form. Norick took those plans
off the shelf and put them into action, and it was through
his efforts to convince the council members and to convince the public that this was the thing that Oklahoma
City needed to step out and become a future destination
city. Because of Ron's personal aura, he had the ability to
get a lot of different classes of people working together. He
was able to get the sports people, the community leaders,
and the arts enthusiasts all to sit down and talk because
he was coming from a focal point that covered all of their
interests. He had interests in a lot of different things, and
that was very valuable in convincing people that also had
similar types of individual interests that they would all fit
in this plan."[13]

One of the first things the group decided on was that they
needed someone to help them through this process. Oklahoma
City had never gone down this road before, and Ron Norick was
ready to start moving. The chamber agreed to raise $25,000 to

start the project rolling. This solved several problems. First, because the money was private the group did not need to go public, and second, because the group had some money they could now hire someone to take them down the road.

In the fall of 1992, Rick Horrow was speaking on sports violence at the University of Oklahoma. Horrow was founder and president of his own consulting company, Horrow Sports Ventures in Miami, Florida. He had consulted on several major projects around the country, mostly sports-related, and specialized in public/private partnerships. Norick was impressed with Horrow, and soon after the appearance at OU, called Horrow and asked him to come to Oklahoma City to talk about some of the issues Oklahoma City was facing and see what he thought.[14]

Norick had also been involved in an earlier meeting with Jim Bruza of Frankfurt Short Bruza and representatives of H.O.K. of Kansas City, Missouri, the largest stadium architectural firm in the country. It was during this meeting that Horrow's name was brought again into the mix. They had been discussing various stadium projects around the country and in doing so, brought up Horrow's name in connection with the Dade County, Florida, stadium work.

The MAPS group decided to conduct interviews so the consultant hiring process would not be misconstrued as a brother-in-law deal, even though there was no requirement to do so since it was funded privately. Three different consulting firms were invited to interview for the consultant work, including Horrow, who would eventually be selected to carry MAPS forward.

The first step was to develop a list of what needed to be accomplished. The group would need to come up with a list of projects that would be included in the proposal to the citizens. The next step Norick wanted to tackle was how best to address the issue.

Should the city propose bond issues, a county-wide sales tax like was passed for United, revenue bonds, Tax Incremental Financing (TIF) tax, or something else? Horrow's assignment was to find out what other combinations of funding were available for this project. The committee brought many ideas as to what was going on around the country in the area of developing public projects, and the one that seemed to make the most sense was a temporary sales tax. The next question was should it be city-wide or county-wide? Because the facilities being addressed were all city-owned facilities, only a city-wide tax would be legally acceptable. Polls indicated that a tax in effect for longer than five years would be considered a permanent tax by the public. So that was the parameter the group would be working with on dollar totals and time needed to bring the money in.

Next was to identify the size of the tax necessary for the projects on the list. This meant coming up with the expected costs for the projects on the list. Jim Bruza of Frankfurt Short Bruza architectural firm in Oklahoma City said his firm would do the estimating and design work at no charge to help in the process. After much discussion, and even arguing at times, an initial list of projects and their costs were identified. There were nine projects at an estimated cost of $236 million. They were as follows: a new baseball stadium, a new arena, a new downtown library/learning center, a canal in Bricktown, a renovated Myriad Convention Center, and Civic Center Music Hall, renovations at the State Fairgrounds, a light-rail/trolley system connecting the areas, and a river project including a series of dams along the North Canadian River. It was estimated that to get $236 million to pay for these projects, it would take a one cent sales tax for 60 months, or five years.

The meetings of the original group had now moved to the level of needing to conduct public business, so the City Council was added to the process as were citizens from the community. Public hearings were conducted where all projects and the financing were reviewed and the recommendations were passed along to the council. Jackie Carey chaired the Council Committee that then moved the project forward.

Next was taking it to the City Council for approval, and to set a ballot date. Norick believed it was crucial to the project that the leaders of the city always be unanimous for the project or it would not go forward, so he worked very closely with the City Council every step of the way, and every vote of importance along the way on MAPS was a unanimous one.

Just as with Norick's first campaign for mayor, there was both good news and bad news on the council approving the list of projects and setting a date. The good news was that on October 13, 1993, they approved it 9-0 and set the date for 60 days out, December 14, 1993. The bad news was that the date of the election was only 60 days away on December 14, 1993, and they had a short time to sell a very big project to the citizens of Oklahoma City. The Oklahoma City Chamber of Commerce raised the money for the campaign to sell the MAPS projects to the voters. They did an exemplary job and raised approximately $365,000, which was a lot of money for a referendum at that time. Norick became the flag-bearer. He believed he had to be out front because if the mayor was not supporting it, why should anyone else?

Early on there was some polling, which told Norick that in order for the projects to be successful, they would have to be voted on as one package, either all up or all down. If taken individually, no single project had enough support to pass. Norick instinctively knew that the folks in the arts community would not kill the sports projects if it also meant killing their projects, and that the sports fans would not kill the arts facilities if it meant killing their facilities. He knew that the only way to make this thing happen was to talk about the big picture of improving Oklahoma City as a whole, not just a small part each individual used. So the ballot was made to be one vote for all nine projects, yes or no. Norick also found out that there seemed to be only one organized opponent to the projects and that was the National Association for the Advancement of Colored People (NAACP). He told the NAACP that a lot of the projects, the arena, the stadium, the convention center, the canal, and the library were in the core and eastern parts of the city, and would be for all the citizens of Oklahoma City. In addition, the council approved several resolutions to contract with small contractors to do as much of the work as possible to allow minority firms a portion of the work.

Another concern that showed up in the polls was that senior citizens would be less likely to vote for MAPS. Norick spoke to senior groups about how the future belonged to their children and grandchildren. This was who the MAPS projects would benefit the most. Also, seniors were told that the city would institute a yearly rebate of approximately $36 to any one over the age of 65 who could produce proof of age and residency in Oklahoma City for the past year. These factors not only neutralized the possible rejection by seniors, but actually encouraged their support.

During the 90-day period prior to the vote, Norick, his assistant Rick Moore, consultant Rick Horrow, and several others went out and sold the idea and concept of MAPS to the voters of Oklahoma City. Norick made it an unstated rule that anywhere they could get two or more people together to hear their pitch, they made it. Frankfort Short Bruza had provided renderings which they used to sell the projects, and the money raised by the chamber had helped produce brochures for distribution.

Ron Norick addresses a crowd outside the Myriad Convention Center during a rally to kick off the campaign for the MAPS project vote. *Courtesy The Daily Oklahoman.*

ABOVE: Brochure used to identify the MAPS projects for the voter and to present the package as a whole. Voters were asked to "Believe in Our Future!" and vote yes on December 14.

RIGHT: Ron Norick raises his hands in celebration as he announces the final numbers of the victory at 54 percent in favor of MAPS. The $238 million project was officially approved by the voters of Oklahoma City on December 14, 1993. *Courtesy The Daily Oklahoman.*

Believe in Our Future!

DECEMBER 14
VOTE YES!

Believe In Our Future ✓ Vote YES Dec. 14

Ron Norick in an 89ers baseball team jersey standing on California Street, dreaming of where the canal and ballpark projects from MAPS will be located. *Courtesy Ron Norick.*

RIGHT: Carolyn Norick, MAPS Consultant Rick Horrow, Ron Norick, Mayor's Assistant Rick Moore, City Council members Willa Johnson, Jack Cornett, Jackie Carey and Mark Schwartz celebrate the MAPS victory on election night at the Bricktown Ballroom. *Courtesy The Daily Oklahoman.*

BELOW: The MAPS Master Plan from the original architectural renderings. *Courtesy Frankfurt Short Bruza.*

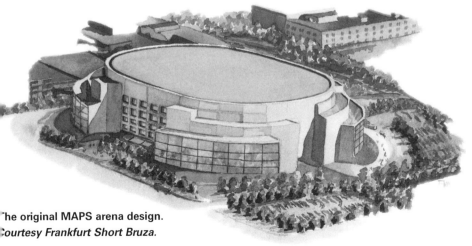

The original MAPS arena design.
Courtesy Frankfurt Short Bruza.

ABOVE: The original canal architectural rendering. Courtesy Frankfurt Short Bruza.

RIGHT: The original Civic Center architectural rendering. Courtesy Frankfurt Short Bruza.

On December 14, 1993, the citizens of Oklahoma City passed the MAPS projects by a 54% / 46% margin, a landslide for a sales-tax increase. That night, as the group celebrated the victory for Oklahoma City's future at the watch party, Norick made the following comments to Moore, "Tonight we passed the vote 54 to 46%, but we have got to remember that over the

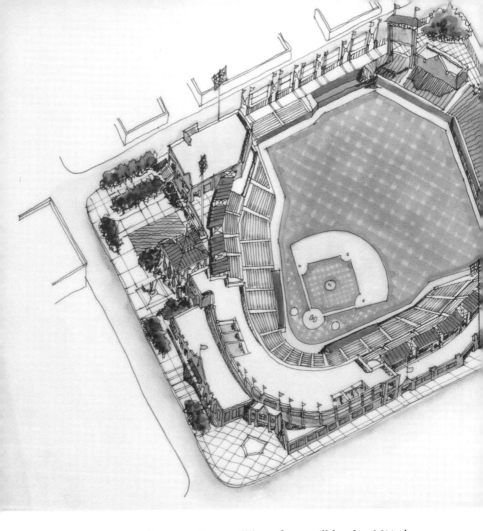

next seven to10 years, all we will hear from will be the 46% that voted against it. We must stay the course and keep our eyes forward on the goal of finishing this job, because I promise you that when it is all over, and the people of Oklahoma City are enjoying these projects, you will be hard pressed to find anyone who voted against it!"

Ten years after this statement, on December 6, 2003, The Daily Oklahoman printed a poll they conducted which asked how citizens voted on MAPS, and the poll showed that 76% said they

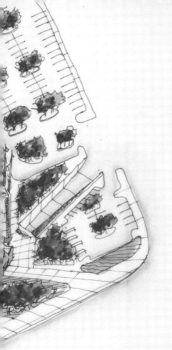

The final ballpark design included several added features such as the center field scoreboard, left field bleachers and the left field restaurant. *Courtesy Anne-Marie Funk, Architectural Design Group.*

voted for MAPS, 89% said they had a favorable opinion of MAPS, and that 88% of those polled said MAPS had changed their opinion of Oklahoma City positively. Ron Norick's prophetic words were proven true.

In November of 2003, Vince Orza, chairman and chief executive of Eateries Inc., former educator, television newsman and gubernatorial candidate, said the following of Norick's leadership in MAPS: "Ten years ago, Oklahoma City Mayor Ron Norick developed a visionary plan to rejuvenate the downtown area. While nearly everyone elected to office seems committed to taking the 'no new taxes' pledge, Norick showed real guts and outstanding leadership by taking just the opposite path."

Norick had persuaded nearly every civic leader, including publisher Edward L. Gaylord and *The Oklahoman*, to support the tax increase. In and of itself, that was perhaps the most amazing display of leadership Oklahoma City had seen in decades. An editorial read, ... "This renaissance is a result of one elected official taking the more difficult and road less traveled to recovery. Ron Norick proposed a well thought out program of projects and spending that has made our city and lives better. Norick distinguished himself by having the guts to lead, execute, and deliver on a promise few other politicians would have even considered. Oklahoma needs more of this type of leadership."[15]

Jim Bruza of the design firm Frankfurt Short Bruza said:

"Ron put everything on the line in my opinion with MAPS, because it was such a bold step. I don't know if I have ever seen a mayor put everything on the line like he did with MAPS. The citizens had demonstrated by other referendums that had already passed that they were willing to pass taxes on themselves, but it had always been for industry. But this was different. It wasn't to bring a business here. People could see the advantages of some of the projects, but nobody seemed to like all nine of the projects. Because of Ron Norick's leadership, it passed. He put a lot of himself into the project and it passed because of him, to a great extent. Ron had this great motto, "Let's leave something for our grandkids." And I thought that was a good way to state it."[16]

Washington, D.C., attorney and former Oklahoma City Ward 2 Councilman Mark Schwartz said of Norick's leadership on MAPS:

"It is easy to make a promise, but often reasonably more difficult to keep. However, it was the Big Promise made in 1993 by then Mayor Ron Norick and the entire city council that was the challenge. Pass the MAPS sales tax and we will build new venues in the city and bring back real convention business to town. We will even have new hotels in Oklahoma City, and we will bring a nightlife to downtown we promised."

"Well, we did it. We made a promise in 1993 and we, together with the MAPS oversight board and subsequent city councils and mayors, kept the promise. But I will always credit Ron Norick for his foresight."

"The simple answer when you look back over 10 years of MAPS from the beginning, without Ron Norick there would be no MAPS. Since Norick left the Mayor's office in 1998, there have been a lot of people try to take some credit for MAPS but the fact of the matter is MAPS was the doing of Ron Norick, and Oklahoma City should remember that forever, because it has affected and will affect the city forever. It is just a simple matter that he is MAPS."[17]

In December of 2003, former Mayor Kirk Humphreys said "Ron Norick put this city on a solid footing with the MAPS projects, and I have worked diligently to build upon the foundation he laid."[18] And so it will be for future mayors of Oklahoma City.

Mayor Ron Norick taking a break during the rescue and recovery efforts
in the days after the bombing of the
Murrah Building seen in the background.
Courtesy The Daily Oklahoman.

CHAPTER XV

APRIL 19, 1995:
The Day that Shocked a Country

IT WAS A SPRINGTIME MORNING IN OKLAHOMA CITY, and more than 1,200 of Oklahoma City's civic, government, and business leaders, along with Mayor Ron Norick, had attended the Mayor's Prayer Breakfast at the Myriad Convention Center in downtown Oklahoma City. The speaker had been Richard L. Fenstermacher, retired marketing director at Ford Motor Company.

Norick left the Myriad about 8:30 a.m. and drove to his office at Grand Centre, located on the east access road to the Hefner Parkway between Northwest 50th Street and Northwest Expressway. He was standing with his dad in his office when at 9:02 a.m. they felt the building shake. Norick's first thought was that a gas line had exploded. He looked out his dad's window, which faces west, and saw people coming out of the building across the street looking in their direction. He quickly ran down the hall to his office, which had a window also facing south, and looked out that window towards downtown. He saw a plume of smoke rising from the skyline and immediately picked up his phone and called City Hall. He spoke to Fran Cory, executive assistant to the Mayor, who said they really had no information there as of yet either, but that there were some windows broken out and offices with ceiling tiles that had fallen to the floor. Fran Cory had been a city employee since 1965, and had been in the mayor's office since becoming Mayor Patience Latting's secretary in 1971. Cory told the mayor that it looked to her like it was coming from the area around the Federal Court House. Ron told Fran that he would wait for her to find out what had happened and return the call to the Norick Investment offices when she knew something.[1]

Members of the press immediately began calling the mayor's office at City Hall to talk to him about the explosion, and Cory was transferring them to Norick Investment. Congressman Ernest Istook, whose office was just three floors above Norick Investment, happened to be in the office when the explosion had occurred, and he came down to find out what Norick knew about the situation. By this time, about 10:00 a.m., Norick decided he needed to be downtown. He had been watching the television reports in his office, and knew the streets around the Alfred P. Murrah Federal Building had been closed off, and people had been urged to stay away from the downtown area.

Norick decided that rather than add to the traffic, he would get Fran Cory to have the police send a car to get him and take him downtown. Soon, two plain clothes policemen arrived to transport the Mayor and the Congressman to City Hall. The two plain clothes officers turned out to be more than just a couple of officers to escort him downtown; they turned out to be his security patrol, because they had by now established the fact that there had been a bomb at a federal building in downtown Oklahoma

City, but they did not know if there were more government targets at the state and local level as well, so they were assigned to the mayor for protection.

When Norick arrived downtown, he immediately went to the police command post, which was located on Broadway Avenue, and walked over to the YMCA and stood on the corner looking at the devastation before him. Cars were still burning and there was activity everywhere as emergency responders and volunteers were scrambling around the perimeter of the building. Norick remembered later how he just stared at where the Murrah Federal Building had been and could not believe it was gone. He noticed lots of smoke, but realized it was from the cars burning, not from the building. He asked the police what had happened, and they told him it was a bomb, but that they did not know much else.

A meeting of all the police, fire, and law enforcement groups was called for 11:00 a.m., at the fire command center which was across the street from the SBC building a few blocks to the north. Norick went to the meeting and observed that Oklahoma City Fire Chief Gary Marrs ran the meeting. Norick remembered how impressed he was with the organization of that meeting. He said, "There was no panic, no indecision, and no question as to what everyone was to do. It was phenomenal that in this kind of situation, one nobody ever expected to be in where a bomb had blown up a building in downtown Oklahoma City, everyone was focused on their job, and everyone was reporting in as to what their unit was doing." The Fire Department was in charge of rescue, the Police Department in securing the area because it was a crime scene, and the Alcohol Tobacco & Firearms & Federal Bureau of Investigation investigating because it was a federal building. Norick was asked to get in touch with Governor Frank Keating, to secure assistance for nighttime security at the Murrah site, with the National Guard and the State Emergency Department. When

Norick reached Governor Keating, he was in the "bunker," where he had been moved immediately after the bombing. The head of the National Guard was with the Governor in the bunker, and of course, Keating said he would do whatever was necessary to help.[2]

Coincidentally, the Mid-Southwest Foodservice Convention was in its second day of a three-day convention at the Myriad when the bombing occurred. There were more than 400 vendors participating in the show, and within an hour of the bombing, they had food out on the site for rescue workers. They had served about 10,000 meals by mid-afternoon on the 19th, and continued to provide meals, as many as 25,000 a day, for rescuers well after their meeting was cancelled.[3]

Norick recalled how the media put out the word that rescuers were working around the clock, and soon people were bringing food and supplies to the security gates for them. In fact, people were bringing supplies by the truck loads at times. When the request went out for wheel barrows to help the rescuers bring things out of the building, there were literally truckloads of wheel barrows brought down to the site by both stores and individuals. It was unbelievable. It was truly the "Oklahoma Standard."

Norick also recalled that the media was, on the whole, very good to work with during the tragedy. There was a daily press conference held at the Civic Center, and Norick told them that he would tell them everything he knew at that time. They also designated spokespeople for each area of the rescue and recovery efforts.

The Oklahoma City Fire Department was the only agency that gave out information relating to number of victims, so there was no conflicting information. They disclosed the basic information, such as if they had found anybody and whether they were dead or alive. If they heard any information from a source other than Chief Gary Marrs or Deputy Fire Chief Jon Hansen, it was not official. On the investigative side, the FBI was responsible for giving out that information.

Norick believed that by having this designated press briefing everyday at the Civic Center it would keep the press away from the site, as well as keeping them informed. He believed that they should tell the press everything they could without giving away things in the law enforcement area. For the most part, the press respected the process because they wanted law enforcement to be able to do their jobs. All information relating to rescue, injuries, and victims, was given to the media as soon as possible after the families were informed. They did not give out names, just numbers.

Norick was impressed with the assistance given by President Bill Clinton's Administration and the federal government, especially people like James Lee Witt, Director of the Federal Emergency Management Agency. Norick said Witt came in that first night and said that he would do everything he could to help and asked what he needed. Norick believed Witt was a real quality guy and he really liked him.

Leon Pannetta, Clinton's Chief of Staff was very helpful, as was Secretary of Housing and Urban Development Henry Cisneros, former mayor of San Antonio, Texas. Norick believed that these people did not work with him as a Democrat or a Republican, but rather as an American mayor of an American city. This opened a lot of doors for Oklahoma City in both the White House and the federal bureaucracy.[4]

The Wednesday after the bombing, Norick was at home resting when about 9:00 p.m. or 9:30 pm the phone rang. When he answered the phone, the voice on the other end identified herself as the White House operator, and asked if he could hold for the

To Rick Moore
With Appreciation,

Bill Clinton

City Councilman Mark Schwartz, Mayor Ron Norick, President
Bill Clinton, Mayor's Assistant Rick Moore, and Oklahoma City's
Washington lobbyist John Montgomery meeting in the Oval Office to
discuss funding for Oklahoma City shortly after the April 19 bombing.
Courtesy Rick Moore.

President. President Clinton got on the phone and asked Norick how he was doing. Clinton was calling from his limo while campaigning in Iowa. He told Norick that he just wanted to let him know he was thinking about him and his city, and if he needed anything, anything at all, to feel free to call him. That call came out of the blue to Norick, and he knew there was nothing political there. It was one leader to another, letting him know he cared.

In the weeks and months following the bombing, Norick made many trips to Washington to visit with members of the government about the bombing, funding, and other things related to the aftermath of the tragedy. On one particular occasion, a few months after the bombing, Norick was in Miami, Florida, addressing the United States Conference of Mayors with a video presentation of how Oklahoma City responded to the bombing. In the audience was Secretary of HUD Henry Cisneros, who after hearing Norick's presentation, asked Norick to come to his room for a meeting. Cisneros said he thought the presentation was powerful, and he would like to get some of that message to Washington so he could help Oklahoma City with some funding from HUD to help rebuild the area around the Murrah Site. He asked Norick if he could come to Washington the next day if he could arrange a meeting with him and President Clinton's Chief of Staff Leon Pannetta. Norick said of course, and within minutes, Cisneros made a phone call to Pannetta and had a meeting with Norick scheduled for the next afternoon.

Norick flew to Washington the next morning. While meeting with Pannetta in the West Wing of the White House, President Clinton called and asked Norick and his entourage to come over to the Oval Office for a visit. Norick, along with his assistant Rick Moore, City Councilman Mark Schwartz, and lobbyist for Oklahoma City John Montgomery, went to the Oval Office and visited with the President for about 30 minutes. The meeting focused on what efforts were being made to help secure federal funding to assist Oklahoma City in its rebuilding of not only the area around the bomb site, but all of downtown. Norick told the President about the MAPS program, which had by this time been more than a year and a half old. The President seemed concerned not just about the brick and mortar, but also about the heart and soul of the people in Oklahoma City. Norick assured the President that the people of Oklahoma City were a hardy and resilient people, and that by combining the strength of their spirit with the strength of their faith, the people of Oklahoma City would rise from the ashes of the Murrah Building and be better than they were before. Again, Clinton and Norick seemed to bond as two leaders who were working together to heal the wounds of April 19.[5]

From the moment he knew what happened, Ron Norick showed the true fabric he was made of by doing everything within his power to help bring Oklahoma City out of this horrific terrorist act. He was tireless in his efforts, catching a quick nap in his office at City Hall. Norick would run home, change clothes, and then come back. He lost his voice, but kept vigil at the site in the driving rains on several nights during the rescue and recovery effort.

Lieutenant Governor Mary Fallin remembered his dedication:

"Taking care of the bombing survivors, looking for the victims, never giving up, and also taking care of the needs of the people in the community, seemed to consume the mayor. He worked with the charities, he worked with the shelters, he worked with the people from out of state who came in to help. I would always see him around. I know I worked a lot of long hours and I know the governor worked a lot of long hours, but I'm not sure Ron Norick even went to bed. He seemed to stay up 24 hours a day, working on the event. And I don't know that everyone had the intensity that he had. He was really intent and devoted to doing all that he could as mayor. As I said before, it was important how we responded because the whole world was watching Oklahoma's reaction, and how we would handle things, and of course, our reaction became known as "The Oklahoma Standard", and part of that image of the Oklahoma Standard came from people like Mayor Ron Norick and his leadership abilities."[6]

He put on a positive face for the national media, and made Oklahoma proud. He dealt with media requests and showed the world the qualities of Oklahomans and their ability to recover from disaster. He supported the rescuers and volunteers by constantly being there for them, patting them on the back, and telling them they were doing a good job. He did not stand back and watch them; he stood with them, and was there for them. He constantly worked to secure funding for Oklahoma City, including taking trips to Washington, D.C., to make the recovery go faster.

Governor Frank Keating put it this way when talking about Ron Norick's leadership qualities during the bombing:

"One thing people don't remember about the Oklahoma City bombing was that Ron Norick wasn't trying to grab the limelight from me or anyone else. Nobody was trying to upstage the other. Ron Norick always worked well with whoever he was placed in contact with. You never had to

ABOVE: United States Senator Don Nickles and Congressman Frank Lucas visit with Ron Norick to discuss funding for Oklahoma City after the Murrah Building bombing. The meeting took place in House Speaker Newt Gingrich's office. *Courtesy Rick Moore.*

BELOW: United States Senator Don Nickles, Mayor Ron Norick, Speaker of the House Newt Gingrich, Governor Frank Keating, Congressman Frank Lucas, and Congressman J.C. Watts at a press conference in the Speaker's office. The topic was funding for Oklahoma City after the Murrah Building bombing. *Courtesy Rick Moore.*

look over your shoulder and worry about what he was going to say or not say. You never had to worry about Ron Norick dropping the ball. I remember when my wife, Cathy, proposed the prayer service after the bombing. A lesser mayor would have said, 'This is my turf, it's at the Oklahoma City Fairgrounds, or I want to chair this, or my wife should be the host. But not Ron Norick. He wasn't interested in who got credit as long as the action took place."[7]

Gary Marrs, who was fire chief of Oklahoma City in 1995 would remember working with Norick during the bombing.

"Many times since the bombing I have had the opportunity to talk about the bombing around the world, I always bring out a couple of things about working with the elected officials. The thing that really helped us in Oklahoma City, that both Sam Gonzales (former Chief of Police and currently in the Dallas office of the FBI) and I agree on is that when Ron and the Council, through Ron's leadership, took the position of staying out of our way. If you will think about it, any of the major cities, New York City for example, where they have had a disaster or incident occur, as you watch it on television, you always see the Mayor or some elected official doing the talking, and that's all you ever see. If you remember back in Oklahoma City, you didn't see Ron very much. I mean he was there, and we never had any doubt that he was going to support whatever we were going to do or give us whatever we needed, but yet he didn't feel the need to get up there and be the front man for all that. In fact, he specifically said from the beginning that I would talk about the rescue, that Sam would talk about the criminal investigation and so on and so forth. That just really helped us do our job."

"That very first morning, during those first hours when we sat down and discussed how we were going to set this thing up, Ron was there with us in the FBI command post, and it was clear to me, and obvious to me, that we had Ron's support. That we had the City's support to do whatever we wanted to do and they would give us whatever we needed, yet he wasn't going to be the front man and certainly, he wasn't going to try to tell us how to do our jobs. He just instilled a confidence in you that he knew and trusted you, and knew you could do a good job, and he was going to support you. And that was just invaluable when you've got an incident like that to handle, it means so much to know that there are things you don't have to worry about, and that is that the Mayor and the other elected officials are not going to get involved in telling you how to run your business."

"If there was a key thing that helped us set what everybody calls the "Oklahoma Standard" and how well the rescue effort was run, that was certainly a key part of it. And Ron set that tone, because then it would have been hard for any of the council people or the city manager and any of his staff people to step up and try to take over when they saw that the mayor was not going to do it. And I think that helped us about as much as anything."

"He also left you with no doubt who was in charge of the City. He just had that aura around him, and he was very encouraging to those of us in the rescue community and the so-called worker bees, so-to-speak, know and understand that."[8]

Former City Councilman Mark Schwartz recalled:
"Ron Norick, as he did with MAPS, showed significant leadership qualities in terms of the tragedy

of April 19, 1995. "Ron played an important role as a spokesperson for the city. He also showed another aspect of leadership when he deferred to others such as the Fire Chief to be responsible for reporting rescue efforts, the police chief to report on the investigation of the crime scene, and on and on.

I think it was also important to note that Ron's leadership in helping pass the 1989 bond issue and the public safety sales tax in 1989 helped enable the fire department to have the additional firefighters, equipment and training to help them do the things they were able to do in the rescue and recovery stage of the bombing. And that impact is still being felt today."[9]

Don Bown, City Manager during that time, remembers:
"The OKC bombing was a major disaster that had never happened in this country relative to a terrorist attack

Ron Norick and City Councilman Mark Schwartz survey some of the devastation after the bombing of the Murrah Building in downtown Oklahoma City. Courtesy Ron Norick.

before that time. We were in what I would say was virgin ground. None of us had done or had experienced what we had just experienced in Oklahoma City at that time. One of the things that was so good about Ron was that during that time, it was his responsibility to keep the council directed in the part that they had in such a thing, and that was to provide the necessary leadership to the city staff to get the things that we needed to resolve the situation at the Murrah Building. So we had regular daily sessions with the Mayor and the Council to go over each day's events. Council was told that this was not a photo op for elected officials, this was a very serious thing, particularly at the beginning, because we didn't know exactly what we were facing. So Ron was particularly strong in that thing in keeping the other elected officials out of the nitty gritty of how do you get this thing under control, how do you get the info out to the public, and how do you do the job of at first seeing if there was anybody else alive in there, how to get the bodies out, how to keep the building from further collapsing, in other words, these were all the things the professionals had to do these things, so I took Police Chief Sam Gonzales, Fire Chief Gary Marrs, and we would meet with mayor Norick and also the council and keep them informed. And I would say that probably in the history of disaster response, this went as well as could be expected it could go. In other words, Ron Norick was not the focal point, but he made sure it was the firemen, the police officers, and other emergency responders and public works people who were really doing the job. In fact, the staff had just come back from a FEMA training session in Maryland where they learned how to deal with disasters, so they really did know what to do, so it was important that we had a Mayor who let those professionals do what they knew how to do. He knew not to get in their way. And if you look at a lot of other places where disasters happen and have happened, you'll see that there are people who use those as a stepping stone to bigger and better offices, and this was not the case in Oklahoma City with Ron Norick. This was truly a very sensitive, very thought-out program and as the elected Mayor of the city, Ron Norick was the face that the city staff used to show the calmness and professionalism that our people had."[10]

Norick had a monthly 30 minute television show on Cox Cable's local access station called "Mayor's Magazine", and the June show was only him narrating a series of slides describing the rescue and recovery efforts from 9:02 a.m. on April 19th until the implosion of the building. He took this video and traveled all over the world showing people the "Oklahoma Standard" he was so proud of. As his Executive Secretary Fran Cory said about him, "Nobody loved Oklahoma City more than Ron Norick."

Andy Burke, Oklahoma City Chamber of Commerce, visits with Norick and the Mayor's Assistant, Rick Moore, as they prepare to land in New York on the "Thank You America" tour after the bombing. *Courtesy Rick Moore.*

CHAPTER XVI

THE LAST TERM

ON SEPTEMBER 7, 1995, A REPORTER for the *Oklahoma Gazette* wrote, "The success or failure of Ron Norick's tenure as mayor of Oklahoma City looked as if it would depend on MAPS, but the April 19 bombing of the federal building changed that outlook considerably."

"You gotta take April 19 and treat it separately," Ron told *The Daily Oklahoman* in a New Year's Day 1996 story. "I know that's hard to do, but if not for the bombing, Oklahoma City had a great, positive year (of 1995)."[1]

That very January, the Bricktown Merchants Association honored Ron at a black-tie event with the very first Golden Brick Award. Citing his commitment to the MAPS project, his tireless promotion for economic growth and always on the lookout for sports developments, the group of 300 celebrated Norick's efforts. When Norick was asked if he thought construction would be finished by the year 2000,

Mayor Ron Norick and his father, Jim, are pleased with the election numbers at the watch party for the 1994 election. This launched Ron's third and final term as mayor. *Courtesy The Daily Oklahoman.*

Norick told them he hoped not. "I want to see lots more construction going on. That will mean the city-funded construction is done and all the private money has kicked in."[2] Just two months earlier, Norick and Rick Moore were in Haikou City, People's

Five generations of Noricks: Ruth Norick (seated left), her son Jim (seated right), his son Ron (standing), Ron's daughter Allyson, and Allyson's baby, Emily in Jim's lap. *Courtesy Ron Norick.*

Republic of China where construction had kicked up dust. Norick told Moore "that's not dust flying through the air, that's progress." He looked forward to seeing that in Oklahoma City.

The success of MAPS was being seen in all aspects of city business. In December of 1995, a $220 million bond issue was passed to make improvements to streets, bridges, traffic control signals, drainage systems, parks, and recreational facilities. The bond issue passed in every ward and the last time this came close to happening was the 1968 "Yes Em-All" campaign handled by Mayor Jim Norick and his secretary at the printing company, Glenda Phillips. Eleven of the twelve propositions passed then.

"I've sensed the attitude of the voter is changing," Ron said at the time. "They are feeling more confident with what is going on at City Hall."

MAPS was fully underway by 1996. All projects were moving ahead either in the planning stage or actual work phase. However, there were times when things came to a complete stop. "I could become your worst nightmare," was the warning Norick gave to architects and engineers when construction bids on the new ballpark came in at $8.4 million higher than projected. The original price tag of $21 million seemed way too low when seven construction firms bid between $28.7 and $30.3 million.[3]

Ron blasted architects for huge conceptual changes to items after they had been approved by City Council. One of those major changes was 36,000 square feet added for a second level concourse for suites, restrooms, and a food court. At that point, Ron gave notice that he would be more active in future MAPS plans. That was the first week of February, 1996. By the middle of the month, Ron became the chief decision-maker for the planning group of MAPS. Their first meeting lasted seven hours that resulted in a revamped plan for the ballpark.

"We're going in a direction that is not going to impede us having a high-quality ballpark with a number of amenities," Ron told the media after the particularly long meeting. "We talked about keeping the ballpark quality, things the 89ers want, things the city wants, and things taxpayers can be proud of."[4]

Even after that tongue-lashing he gave the architects over the ballpark, Norick was honored by the American Institute of Architects Central Oklahoma Chapter. He was given a special award for his "dedication to improving the quality of life in Oklahoma City." Good moments like this and humorous moments like the Gridiron Banquet helped everyone get through those stressful times. Jerry Howard of the University of Oklahoma portrayed Ron in the Gridiron that year as a "Mr. Rogers" character talking about "my town the penny sales tax built."[5]

When the federal trials for Timothy McVeigh and Terry Nichols were moved to Denver, Colorado, Ron announced that, "I'm very disappointed for the families. I think they have the right to have this trial here." He immediately made plans to provide help with family members' living expenses in Denver while the trials were held. The $1.2 million in the Mayor's Disaster Relief Fund would help.

President Clinton returned again to Oklahoma City on April 5 to meet with the victims and families on the first anniversary of the bombing. He would be out of the country on April 19, but wanted to visit before he left. The President and the First Lady spent all afternoon at three sites visiting with families and survivors. On April 19, Vice President Al Gore accompanied Governor Frank Keating and Mayor Ron Norick to services at the Myriad Convention Center. In speaking to the media at a press conference in the Medallion Hotel, Norick addressed concerns over the economic impact the bombing had on the city. "We've learned it will cost about $65 million to rebuild that area. I wrote the President and I will forward that request to Congress." Federal aid totaled about $39 million up to this point, so Norick was asking for another $26 million to overcome the damage and loss.[6]

An uplifting experience occurred one week later when the Oklahoma City Blazers Hockey team brought home the Central Hockey League championship. Joe Burton, captain of the team, said, "It's been a hard year for everybody, but hopefully bringing this championship to the city will help them feel better." He added, "What we did is not going to change what happened there is nothing we can do to make them forget a catastrophe like that but maybe for a day people can come out and have a little fun." Coach Doug Sauter offered, "I know what we did was a very, very small thing compared to what happened here a year ago. But there were an awful lot of smiling faces out there today. It is something I will not forget for a long time." As a life-long hockey fan, Ron Norick was there for much of the season. It was a satisfying moment and a nice distraction for him as well.

Another distraction, maybe not as nice, during Norick's time as mayor was the on-going saga of restoration of the Skirvin Hotel. By April of 1996, a year had passed since Indonesian businessman Oesman Sapta had purchased the stately old hotel for $1.7 million. Sapta was being sued by an ex-employee of his used car dealership on North May Avenue. With little to no activity going on at the Skirvin, speculation began again about whether this owner would do anything with it or not.

Even more close to home, renovation had begun on City Hall. Everyone was being moved around so that work could proceed in a more timely manner. Even the council chambers were under construction causing meetings to be held elsewhere. Norick's office was moved to the basement of the Civic Center.

On February 27, Ron Norick testified before a United States House subcommittee in Washington, D.C., searching for $13 million in federal funds to help pay for the light rail system portion of MAPS. This rail would connect the airport to the hotels on I-40 and South Meridian east to downtown and Bricktown and possibly on to the State Capitol, then to the Oklahoma City Zoo/Remington Park area.

In July of 1996, Senator Don Nickles and Senator Jim Inhofe got $10 million included in a transportation spending bill to help pay for the MAPS transit system. Congressman Frank Lucas testified before a House Appropriations subcommittee to secure money for the transit system, but had no luck.

Congressman Ernest Istook said, "I have some skepticism that has to do with the number of riders that would use the system." He had seen estimates of 600 to 700 people a day and that would not increase much over 20 years. "The question is whether we should spend that kind of money to serve that number of people and whether that qualifies as mass transit."[7]

Istook's skepticism came to a head in September when an article in *The Daily Oklahoman* proclaimed that, "Opposing other Oklahoma lawmakers and Oklahoma City officials, Rep. Ernest Istook has told a key House appropriator that the federal government shouldn't spend money on a downtown rail system for the MAPS project." Istook said, "I do not believe this project is cost-justified, or a proper use of U.S. taxpayers' money under the guise of 'mass transit.'" Istook sent a two-page letter to Representative Frank Wolf, chairman of the House Appropriations subcommittee on transportation, faulting the light rail proposal on several fronts.[8]

Norick told *The Daily Oklahoman* that Istook "took me aside and said he would not oppose the plan or the request for federal money. Then, as the Mayor put it, he blindsided me."[9] Istook said that no elected official should try to get a job done by relying on someone else to keep quiet. As a result, the MAPS light rail proposition died. It would be the only portion of the plan passed by the voters of Oklahoma City to not succeed. One year later, Istook secured $1.6 million to buy the trolley buses he felt would work better than the light rail.

The summer of 1996 was a busy sports time for Oklahoma City and Ron Norick. On July 25, the Oscar J. Boldt Construction Company submitted the lowest bid of $21.6 million to build the new ballpark. "We've got a ballpark, folks," Norick proclaimed at the end of the bid openings. "We're thrilled. We've got a really well-designed ballpark that the people are going to be very happy with. I'm very pleased with the construction community that got out and sharpened their pencils."

That same month, the Oklahoma Sports Commission received an invitation to apply for a National Hockey League relocation and expansion franchise. "They don't invite just everybody and it's the first step in the process," Ron said. A rally was called in front of the Myriad and 500 people showed up to be part of an effort called, "NHL Now!" The rally was videotaped to be played for the NHL's Board of Governors when the Oklahoma City group made its pitch for a franchise. Nashville, Tennessee, Atlanta, Georgia, and Houston, Texas, were also joining in the hunt.

In the fall, more good sporting news arrived. Because of the MAPS improvements to the fairgrounds, the American Quarter Horse Association announced that its annual World Championship Show would remain in Oklahoma City for a number of years. When it was Norick's turn to speak to the group at the National Cowboy and Western Heritage Museum where the announcement was made, he said, "Economically, you can talk to the hotel and restaurant people and they know when the quarter horse people are in town. They're quality people. And they stay here for 14 days."[10] Obviously he was pleased.

By December, the preliminary design for the new arena was released. With a nod to Bricktown, it had a rustic charm and a price tag of $84 million. At the same time, the Jim Norick Arena at the State Fairgrounds had received approval of contracts to renovate the 31-year old structure.

BELOW: The grand entrance area to the ballpark can be seen in this early summer of 1997 photo. Soon, the smell of hotdogs and popcorn would fill the air as the Bricktown Ballpark opened for the next season. *Courtesy Bill Moore.*

RIGHT: In this view looking west on California Street toward the Myriad, the brick street can be seen where the future path of the canal would take. *Courtesy Bill Moore.*

As the steel went up on the ballpark in the winter of 1997, the citizens of Oklahoma City could see the first of the MAPS projects taking shape. The grandstands can be seen in this photo looking southwest. *Courtesy Bill Moore.*

ABOVE: Excavation would dig this dirt away and place the canal below street level heading south at this point west of the ballpark. *Courtesy Bill Moore.*

RIGHT: By winter of 1997, the dirt was being hauled away and the canal was taking shape. This is looking west on what once was California Street. *Courtesy Bill Moore.*

ABOVE: On July 4, 1999, the grand opening of the Bricktown Canal was attended by thousands. One of the more anticipated venues of MAPS, the canal added to the beauty of this new recreation area of downtown Oklahoma City. *Courtesy Bill Moore.*

As the new year began, Norick, with Clayton I. Bennett at his side, and the Oklahoma Sports Commission made their pitch to the NHL. He promoted Oklahoma City by saying that various cable and television stations wanted airing rights, a number of season tickets had already been sold, and the whole state would serve as the fan base.

To avoid a conflict or perception of impropriety, the Mayor eliminated himself as a future investor in an NHL franchise. Obviously, this was a big sacrifice for him and his love of the game. Bennett remarked that, "He has been a part of hockey in this community and has a real interest in it. But the big picture is we all need this [the

LEFT: The Ford Center Arena opened in June 2002. After its first year of operation, it was listed among the top ten money grossing facilities in the world. *Courtesy Rick Moore.*

BELOW: In December of 1999, the arena started growing from the ground up. In this view looking north toward downtown Oklahoma City, the concrete is seen taking shape around the steel rebar. *Courtesy Bill Moore.*

granting of the franchise] to happen. If we need to remove any conflict barriers, perceived or otherwise, we should do that. I applaud him for standing up in the role of mayor and working with us."[11]

On April 9, 1997, NHL Commissioner Gary Bettman and the NHL Expansion Committee arrived in Oklahoma City to spend five hours discussing Oklahoma City as a potential NHL city. While other potential cities had provided pep rallies and banners, Norick decided to keep it all business. As Mark Schwartz put it, "These folks are in town for a very short period of time and they want to see what this city has to offer." Afterwards, Bettman said, "We saw a substantive, impressive presentation. I speak for the Board of Governors when I say we have a lot of positive things to report back to the full ownership group."[12]

In June, the NHL announced its new expansion cities and Oklahoma City was not among them. Most agreed that it was the weak size of the television market in Oklahoma City. The lowest of all cities considered, Oklahoma City ranked 43rd nationally. As usual, the Mayor saw a positive side when he said, "I think we enhanced our exposure quite a bit nationally. This community is being viewed differently…in a very positive light. We might have distinguished ourselves more than any other city."

On June 3, Norick attended groundbreaking ceremonies for the YMCA child-care center to replace the one lost in the former location across from the Murrah Building. He told the gathering that the community was affected profoundly by the bombing. "The children are the ones who affected us the most. We can renew our spirits, we can have a new place for our children to learn…in a safe environment. This is going to be a wonderful place."[13]

By July 2, the Oklahoma City Memorial Foundation had selected the winning design for the Bombing Memorial. It was submitted by Torrey Butzer, her husband Hans-Ekkehard Butzer, and Sven Berg of Locus Bold Design in Austin, Texas. Torrey was a native of Oklahoma. At the announcement of the winning design, Mayor Norick said, "I remember when I first met with the committee two years ago. I looked out then on the faces of a very sad and bitter community, one that didn't understand what happened. When I looked back out over them last night, I saw a little bit of hope in their eyes."[14]

In August, Norick threw out the first pitch for the final baseball game to be played in All Sports Stadium, the very park that Mayor Jim Norick had initiated with a first pitch on the evening of April 19, 1962. It was the end of an era and the beginning of a whole new ballgame to change to the Bricktown Ballpark next season.

MAPS had established itself as a successful venture without one major venue open yet. The word had spread across the country and the call for Norick to speak about it came from other cities interested in how he did it. The Mayor remembered that at the first meeting, Rick Moore had come up with the acronym MAPS for Oklahoma City use. In Hampton Roads, Virginia, officials had coined MAPS to mean Metropolitan Area Projects Strategies and asked Norick to come speak to them. They even hired Rick Horrow to be their consultant as well. Horrow told them that "Oklahoma City did something very special. It will stand the test of history."[15]

With such success, what could Norick do for an encore? Apparently, there was some talk that he might not run for a fourth term as mayor. Mark Schwartz, Jerry Foshee, and Guy Liebmann all waited to hear his decision, admitting they were interested in the job. But no one wanted to run against the Mayor. Norick himself had said, "I sure wouldn't want to leave and then MAPS not be done right." He felt it was progressing, but added, "What I'm trying to decide is if everything is in place. Is everything going to be done the way I think it should be done?" Jerry Foshee said, "You don't switch horses in the middle of the stream." Mark Schwartz admitted, "I wouldn't run against Ron. We've served together 10 years now."

Norick was reflecting on his 10 years as mayor. He oversaw the passage of a public safety tax to help police and fire protection. The largest bond issue in the city's history of $220 million was passed to help rebuild streets and parks. MAPS was perhaps the most satisfying of all. He would always remember the Murrah Building bombing and the recovery by a city and a nation.

SBC Bricktown Ballpark.
Photo courtesy of the Oklahoma Redhawks Baseball Club.

City Manager Don Bown beat Ron to it by announcing his retirement after a distinguished career with the city. Assistant City Manager Glenn Deck was quickly selected to replace him. "Whenever we've had a vacancy," Norick said, "a city manager has either left because he was going to work somewhere else or

In this aerial from 2001, the partially roofed arena can be seen with a completed ballpark and canal. The remake of this warehouse district breathed new life into downtown Oklahoma City. *Courtesy Bill Moore.*

had been fired. We've never had the luxury of being able to have an orderly transition. But that's what we expect to happen now."

At an October 29 news conference, Ron Norick, announced he would not seek re-election. In 1991 he won his first re-election with 80 percent of the vote. In 1994 he won with more than 70 percent against several opponents. In 1990 Ron returned $37,000 to campaign donors and in 1994, he sent back $10,200. "There wasn't any reason to leave dollars laying in a bank account," he reasoned.[16] Guy Liebmann said, "His honest, dedicated leadership is just phenomenal."[17] As soon as he had made his plans known, Norick announced he would lead the effort for a short extension of the MAPS sales tax. The extra money would be needed to finish the job right. "I wouldn't mind taking the heat on this," Ron said. "It would be my final hurrah."

As he prepared to leave office, Norick was dealing with future Oklahoma city needs. He worked to support the revitalization efforts of Automobile Alley on North Broadway. He began the process to get the I-40 Crosstown relocation project fully funded. He also saw the early private investments begin to pay off from

MAPS when John Q. Hammons agreed to build a $40 million hotel downtown.

At the end of January, 1998, about 500 people came to the National Cowboy and Western Heritage Museum to pay tribute to this most popular Mayor. And on April 14, 1998, Mayor Ron Norick became plain citizen Ron Norick as Kirk Humphreys was sworn in as Oklahoma City's 34th Mayor. Later that year, the MAPS tax extension was approved by voters 2 to 1. On July 1, 1999, the original MAPS tax and the tax extension ended as promised.

EPILOGUE

OKLAHOMA CITY HAS BEEN BLESSED with the right leaders at the right time. Jim Norick returned from the battles of the South Pacific during World War II to serve his hometown. The men who came before him helped forge this city into the stable, strong metropolitan area we know today as Oklahoma City. Mayors with names like William Couch, Edward Overholser, John C. Walton, Robert Hefner, and Allen Street led the way in the first half of the 20th Century. Jim and Ron Norick would guide the central Oklahoma community through the second half.

Jim began his political life in the spring of 1951 with the campaign for City Council. Serving as mayor from 1959 to 1963 and again from 1967 to 1971, Jim was involved in the operation of Oklahoma City during the three decades of the 1950s, 1960s and 1970s. Ron began his campaign for mayor in the spring of 1987. His service as mayor until 1998 covered the decades of the 1980s and 1990s. And today, Ron still works with his inspiration called MAPS as chairman of the River Project.

For more than 50 years the Norick name has been trusted by the citizens of Oklahoma City. They knew that their government was in good hands. Mick Cornett recognized that strength when he asked Jim to perform his swearing-in ceremony as mayor on March 2, 2004.

Jim served a total of 12 years in office, eight as mayor and four on the

Ron Norick speaking at the opening of the new Ronald J. Norick Downtown Library in 2004. The Library was the final capital project from the MAPS program. *Courtesy Rick Moore.*

City Council. Ron served 11 years as mayor, two 4-year terms and a 3-year term during a charter change for the office.

The city limits expanded dramatically under Jim's watch. Oklahoma City at one point became the largest city in acreage of any in the world. Mindful of this expansion and the problems of the Dust Bowl just a few decades before, Jim saw to it that water would be available for Oklahoma City. Lake Atoka, Lake Stanley Draper, and the 90-mile pipeline between the two provided for an ample supply. McGee Creek, begun under Jim, was completed under Ron's watch.

When providing infrastructure for the citizens of a community, streets, sewers, and basic needs are crucial and the Noricks made sure those important areas were taken care of. Something else both Jim and Ron also saw as very important was providing for the citizen's recreation. Parks and playgrounds were basic to that. However, large gathering facilities also are needed. The Myriad Convention Center was completed under Jim's second term as mayor with the dedication on November 5, 1972 and before he left office, the Fairgrounds Arena was named for him. In its first year of existence, the Ford Center Arena was listed by Pollstar, the concert industry's exclusive in-depth research group, among the top ten money grossing facilities in the world. The 2003 analysis showed the Ford Center Arena at number 10 on the list behind Quebec, England, and New York's Madison Square Garden which came in at number seven. The City Council renamed the portion of Robinson Avenue that runs by the Cox Center and the Ford Center as Ronald J. Norick Boulevard. On the day of the Ronald J. Norick Downtown Library grand opening, Ron admitted to being a little nervous. "It's pretty humbling, it really is," he

observed before the event. It was very appropriate that the last of the MAPS projects would bear the name of the man who made it a reality. On August 17, 2004, dignitaries joined together to pay tribute to Ron at the new four story, 110,000 square foot library. Fred Hall called Ron the "Master Developer" of MAPS. Mayor Mick Cornett also spoke of this being a time to officially declare the completion of MAPS. As City Manager Jim Couch said, "MAPS has obviously led to a lot of positive things for downtown and Oklahoma City in general…This has been a historic period of growth."[1]

Leadership above all things was critical to the Norick methodology. It was not a planned or outlined process. Both men were called on in times of trouble and both responded to the call. During the time of national anxiety and strife, when racial riots rocked our nation, Jim's leadership helped maintain a calm

Ronald J. Norick Do
Metropolitan Library Syste

ABOVE: The Norick family gathered for the dedication of the Norick Library, from left to right: Ron and wife, Kandy, Emily Frosaker and Caroline Waldron (Ron's granddaughters), Allyson (Ron's daughter), Kelly McLaughlin (Kandy's son), Jim and Madalynne, Alex and Angie Koumaris (Jim's grandson, Vickie's son and his wife), Vickie (Jim's daughter, Ron's sister), and Mike Waldron (Caroline's father). *Courtesy Rick Moore.*

RIGHT: Mayors Jim and Ron Norick in front of the new "Ronald J. Norick Downtown Library" at the grand opening on August 17, 2004. Both men were architects of a better lifestyle in Oklahoma City. Courtesy Rick Moore.

in Oklahoma City. Three decades later, when a truck bomb was detonated in downtown Oklahoma City, Ron's leadership helped the citizens of this city and the citizens of the world stand tall and together.

Jim was the first Oklahoma City-born mayor and Ron was the first son of a mayor to be mayor. Ron also closed out the first century of Oklahoma City's existence as mayor in 1989 and gave the city a firm foundation as it began its second hundred years. Both Jim and Ron began their civic involvement with the Oklahoma City Junior Chamber (Jaycees). They both moved on as active Chamber members and both moved from there into politics.

ABOVE: The Norick family gathered at the Oklahoma City Public Schools Foundation ceremony honoring Jim and Madalynne in October of 1992. Left to right are Vickie, Ron, Madalynne, and Jim Norick. *Courtesy The Daily Oklahoman.*

LEFT: Madalynne and Jim Norick at the Oklahoma City University Distinguished Service Awards Ceremony. On April 4, 1991, Jim was recognized for his support of the arts and the university. *Courtesy Jim Norick.*

中华人民共和国海南省海口市
美利坚合众国俄克拉荷马州俄克拉荷马市 缔结
SIGNING CEREMONY FOR THE ESTABLISHMENT OF A SISTER CITY RELATIONSHIP BETWEEN
REPUBLIC OF CHINA, AND OKLAHOMA CITY, OKLAHOMA, THE UNITED STATES OF A

In May, 1992, Norick Brothers Printing was sold to their major competitor, Reynolds and Reynolds. They had tried several times through the years to either buy Norick Brothers or run them out of business. The price and time was finally right.

After Jim left office in 1971, he was elected the Director General of the 1971 Central State Shrine Association where more than 7,500 Shriners attended. Jim was a past Potentate of the India Temple in Oklahoma City. He appeared in Who's Who in America in 1972 and was appointed to the board of directors of Central National Bank in 1973. He also served on the Water Resources Board for Governor George Nigh from 1980 to 1987. In 1991, Jim was honored with a Distinguished Service Award

LEFT: Ron Norick signs a sister city agreement with the mayor of Haikou City, Hainan Province in the People's Republic of China. Looking on are Oklahoma City businessmen Chris Kauffmann, Dr. Hong-Yih Chang, and Assistant to the Mayor Rick Moore. *Courtesy Rick Moore.*

BELOW: Pope Paul VI greets Jim and Madalynne on their trip to the Vatican in 1970. Although they weren't of the Catholic faith, the Noricks felt honored to meet the Pope. *Courtesy Jim Norick.*

RIGHT: Ron Norick and Rick Moore in Tianamon Square in Beijing, People's Republic of China. The Forbidden City can be seen in the background. This was part of a Sister's Cities trip to Haikou. *Courtesy Rick Moore.*

BELOW: Ron Norick surveys the Great Wall of China in one of his trips to that Asian country in November of 1995. *Courtesy Rick Moore.*

Enjoying his retirement from public office, Ron Norick and his wife, Kandy, continue to be involved in the civic life of Oklahoma City. Together, they are enjoying the fruits of his efforts to make Oklahoma City a destination point. *Courtesy Ron Norick.*

from Oklahoma City University. He was instrumental in making the Norick Art Center a reality.

Jim has traveled extensively representing Oklahoma City. He met with the President of Israel on a trip to that country. He had a private audience with the Pope in Rome. He was given an extended tour of the White House by Oklahoman Bryce Harlow and he worked with several United States Presidents.

When Ron Norick took office in 1987, the City of Oklahoma City had two "Sister City" relationships: Taipei, Taiwan, and Tainan, Taiwan. When he left office in 1998, Oklahoma City had six "Sister City" relationships, adding four during his tenure: Haikou, People's Republic of China, Puebla, Mexico, Yehud, Israel, and Ulyanovsk, Russia. Ron believed that through these sister city relationships, we could learn more about each other, as well as encourage more business and educational relationships. Ron was always sure to add education exchanges to the cities' agreements, as well as business and cultural exchanges. There were several education exchanges between the various sister cities and Oklahoma City, using many of the local universities' faculty members. There were also secondary sister school relationships between Oklahoma City schools and schools in these sister cities, where students would exchange letters and artwork.

In each of these cities, there were Oklahoma City businesspeople and educational institutions interested in each other that helped make each city's selection work. For example, in Haikou, People's Republic of China, there was a business relationship with Star Manufacturing Co. in Oklahoma City, as well as relationships between Hainan University and Oklahoma City University and the University of Central Oklahoma. In Ulyanovsk, Russia, St. Lukes United Methodist Church, under the leadership of Pastor Bob Long, was establishing a sister church in the Russian community and was having doctors and others from their church make trips to Russia taking supplies. In Yehud, Israel, there was an exchange between OCU and a university in Israel of music students, which had Israeli band members traveling to Oklahoma City and play concerts here for Oklahoma City audiences. While the students could not talk the same language with their mouths, they could talk the same language with their musical instruments.

Ron traveled to these cities to personally establish the relationships, and felt strongly that by working with people of other countries, he could help Oklahoma City become a global community both economically and culturally.

When Ron left office in 1998, he may have retired from the office of mayor, but he certainly did not retire from being an active part of Oklahoma City and its continued advancement as a major city. He served as Finance Chairman for the 2000 Bond Issue in Oklahoma City called "More Progress Without More Taxes," which passed by the largest margin of victory of any bond issue in Oklahoma City's history, and was also the largest bond issue in Oklahoma City's history at more than $340 million.

In March of 2001, Norick was unanimously approved to the position of chairman of the Oklahoma City Riverfront Redevelopment Authority, which is responsible for overseeing all city-owned land along the corridor of the North Canadian River.[2]

In this position, Norick will help lead the City's efforts to develop the river not only with the MAPS projects on the river, but all economic development projects, such as the Native American Cultural Center.[3] Ron also did not retire from the business world. He is managing principal of Norick Investments, a family investment and development company, and in 1998, he joined advertising executives Larry Bledsoe and Mike McAuliffe to form a new advertising agency called Bledsoe Norick McAuliffe Advertising.[4]

ABOVE:This is the first in a series of dams on the North Canadian River later to be renamed the Oklahoma River along this seven mile stretch. These dams provided a bank-to-bank water flow, setting in place the development of the riverfront property. *Courtesy Anne-Marie Funk.*

He also was involved in a racing partnership with his son, Lance, called L&R Motorsports, a company that owned two teams that raced in the NASCAR Craftsman Truck Series. When Ron left office in 1998, he said, "I am really not going to be sitting around on my hands. It is just going to be a lot easier to do that and have a little time with the family. Now, at least, I don't have to revolve my life around Tuesdays."[5]

Jim and Ron Norick, are forever indelibly linked with Oklahoma City. Without the Noricks, Oklahoma City would not be where it is today, and if you ask the Noricks, without Oklahoma City, they would not be where they are today. The Noricks of Oklahoma City truly are trackmakers in the history of this community.

Ron's son, Lance, is a regular in the NASCAR Craftsman Truck Series. L&R Motorsports is a racing partnership between Lance and Ron, sponsoring two teams in the NASCAR truck series. Courtesy Kaye Olsmith.

MAYORS OF OKLAHOMA CITY

(From a List Compiled by Louise Painter)

COUCH, WILLIAM L.	April 27, 1889 to November 11, 1889
BEALE, ANDREW JACKSON	November 27, 1889 to December 30, 1889
GIBBS, D.W.	July 15, 1890 to August 9, 1890
GAULT, W.J.	August 12, 1890 to April 12, 1892
MITSCHER, O.A.	April 23, 1892 to April 9, 1894
BUTTON, NELSON	April 9, 1894 to April 13, 1896
JONES, CHARLES GRAHAM	April 13, 1896 to April 12, 1897; and April 8, 1901 to April 13, 1903
ALLEN, J.P.	April 12, 1897 to April 10, 1899
VAN WINKLE, LEE	April 10, 1899 to April 8, 1901; and April 13, 1903 to April 10, 1905
MESSENBAUGH, J.G.	April 10, 1905 to April 8, 1907
SCALES, HENRY M.	April 8, 1907 to April 11, 1910
LACKEY, DAN V.	April 11, 1910 to June 8, 1911

GRANT, WHIT M.	June 8, 1911 to April 13, 1915
OVERHOLSER, EDWARD	April 13, 1915 to December 24, 1918
SHEAR, BYRON D.	December 25, 1918 to April 7, 1919
WALTON, JOHN CALLOWAY	April 7, 1919 to January 9, 1923
DONNELLY, MIKE	January 9, 1923 to April 4, 1923
CARGILL, O.A.	April 4, 1923 to April 12, 1927
DEAN, WALTER C.	April 12, 1927 to April 12, 1931
BLINN, C.J.	April 12, 1931 to November 7, 1933
MCGEE, TOM	November 7, 1933 to April 9, 1935
MARTIN, JOHN FRANK	April 9, 1935 to April 11, 1939
HEFNER, ROBERT A.	April 11, 1939 to April 8, 1947
STREET, ALLEN	April 8, 1947 to April 7, 1959
NORICK, JAMES H.	April 7, 1959 to April 9, 1963; and April 11, 1967 to April 13, 1971
WILKES, DR. JACK S.	April 9, 1963 to May 3, 1964
SHIRK, GEORGE H.	June 16, 1964 to April 6, 1965; and April 6, 1965 to April 11, 1967
LATTING, PATIENCE	April 13, 1971 to April 12, 1983
COATS, ANDY	April 12, 1983 to April 14, 1987
NORICK, RONALD J.	April 14, 1987 to April 14, 1998
HUMPHREYS, KIRK	April 14, 1998 to Nov. 3, 2003
LIEBEMAN, GUY *(interim)*	Nov. 3, 2003 to March 2, 2004
CORNETT, MICK	March 2, 2004 to present

JAMES NORICK TIME LINE

1959 to 1963 and 1967 to 1971 Mayoral Terms

1959 TO 1963 MAYORAL TERM

April 7, 1959

James Norick is sworn in as mayor of Oklahoma City.

August 25, 1960

Mayor Norick attended a special welcome home celebration for Jerrie Cobb. She was returning to Oklahoma City after being selected to begin a program at NASA to possibly become the first woman in space.

August 29, 1960

The federal government asked Oklahoma City to build a civil aero-medical research building at the cost of $2.5 million at Will Rogers Field.

September 27, 1960

Land was purchased for the southeast side of the airport from George and Grace Rogers. It was located south of Southwest 74th between Portland and Meridian Avenues.

November 13, 1960

An unusual dedication had Mayor Norick cutting the ribbon to the first family-type fallout shelter at the main entrance of Lincoln Park Zoo, about 150 feet south of Monkey Island.

December 2, 1960

Mayor Norick attended the premiere of the movie "Cimarron" at the Midwest Theater. Glenn Ford, Maria Schell, and Anne Baxter, stars of the film, were on hand.

December 7, 1960

City Council approved plans for a shopping mall between Northwest 23rd and Northwest 30th Streets called the Shepherd Plaza shopping center.

December 13, 1960

Mayor Norick participated in groundbreaking activities with Governor Edmondson of two new State office buildings.

April 16, 1961

Mayor Norick attended a ribbon-cutting ceremony at 2701 Southwest 29th Street for the New York firm Atlantic Mills Thrift Department Store. One of 27 across the nation, this 70,400 square foot store cost $600,000.

May 1, 1961

The first jet passenger service came to Oklahoma City when a TWA Convair 880 landed at Will Rogers Field from San Francisco headed to New York City.

May 8, 1961

Madalynne Norick donned noise-suppression earmuffs and with two golden batons, signaled the start-up for American Airlines first jet flight service for Oklahoma City. This came after the Mayor made the announcement, "American Airline flight 27 inaugural 707 jet flagship for Dallas and Los Angeles may now be boarded at gate seven. All aboard please."

June 27, 1961

Mayor Norick was empowered to appoint a five member urban renewal commission in June of 1961. Norick said he would do his best to keep politicians off of the commission.

July 14, 1961

It was announced that Triple-A professional baseball would be coming to Oklahoma City in April of 1962. A new $275,000 park would be built at the northwest corner of the fairgrounds.

July 9, 1961

Baseball had been missing from Oklahoma City since 1958 when the Texas League franchise was moved to Corpus Christi. Houston's jump to the Major League left an opening for a new Triple-A team and that would be in Oklahoma City.

July 27, 1961

Mayor Norick called council to a meeting in the city manager's office to determine what type of trust system would be used to finance the stadium construction.

July 27, 1961

"We must get men of integrity, men who have the best interests of the city at heart." Mayor Norick spoke these words in describing his search for the members of the newly created Urban Renewal Authority.

August 9, 1961

The fall street bond issue was getting out of hand. Council members had added projects on to the original $10.5 million street bond issue to bring it up to a whopping $55 million. "The people will not buy such a large bond issue at this time," Norick said, "but they will vote for street improvements." He then threw his support behind just the original street bond issue and none of the add-ons.

The city council had changed in the previous spring election and had a five to three split on most issues. Norick usually sided with the three. "There has been a lot said about public opinion and lack of confidence in city government. In my opinion I don't think this so-called confidence is any better than when the four new councilmen were elected last spring."

August 13, 1961
The Sunday Oklahoman editorial supported Norick's position on the bond money. "Far more disturbing," the editorial read, "is the possibility that the often unpredictable council majority may be led to act in some instances more out of a spirit of personal vindictiveness than in keeping with the city's best interests."

August 15, 1961
The council voted to send a $55 million bond to a vote of the people. The bond would include $2.5 million for right of way, $9.1 million for streets, $17 million for sanitary sewers, $7.5 million for storm sewers, $5.25 million for parks, $4 million for police, $3 million for fire, $1 million for libraries, and $6 million for airports. Each item would be voted on separately. Doubts were

expressed by the editorial page as to the wisdom of lumping too many proposed improvements together in one proposal.

August 16, 1961
Architects Wright & Selby were selected to design the new baseball park at the fairgrounds.

August 22, 1961
Tulakes Airport may get a new name at the suggestion made at city council to rename the airport after Wiley Post. Ed Moler, city attorney, was asked to draw up a resolution to that effect. It was voted on and approved at the September 5 meeting.

August 25, 1961
By the next council meeting, the bond issue was pared down from $55 to $38 million, reducing several of the categories.

August 30, 1961
With the council bickering over the bond issue as well as trying to replace a city manager who resigned, Norick called on the councilmen to "quit this schoolboy bickering and come to an agreement. There are two very important items before the council at the present time, namely a bond issue to be decided and the re-entry of Oklahoma City into professional baseball ranks. Certainly it is very necessary that a park for the baseball program be completed within the next six months. Perhaps each of the councilmen should be reminded that although he was elected by the people of his ward, he has taken an oath to serve all the people of Oklahoma City, and not a certain

group. The good and well being of Oklahoma City is at stake and should be placed above any petty, personal or political conflicts."

September 1, 1961

The council acted and voted the $39 million bond issue to a vote of the people.

September 10, 1961

Madalynne Norick spent a lot of time volunteering with the Red Cross. She and another volunteer, Lyle Ramsey, described in a newspaper article that, "You don't have to be an expert to be a Red Cross volunteer." The article was calling for volunteers to attend an orientation class.

September 10, 1961

Still going strong in the Municipal League, Madalynne served as chairman of women's activities for the statewide convention held in Oklahoma City in September.

October 6, 1961

The official announcement for the Triple-A baseball team came. Mayor Norick signed the agreement and set out to name the new club through a contest.

October 10, 1961

Plans for a new Oklahoma Science and Arts Foundation planetarium structure at the Fairgrounds was announced by John Kirkpatrick.

October 22, 1961

Mayor Norick and Mrs. Wiley Post unveiled the bust of Wiley Post as the Tulakes Airport was renamed in his honor.

October 25, 1961

All nine bond issues pass.

November 1, 1961

Meanwhile, Norick's five names for the Urban Renewal Authority: Rev. Hugh Bumpass, Dean Willis Wheat, Mrs. Frank Hightower, Leo O'Brien, and Edgar Van Cleef, were put on hold by the city council as they wanted input on it.

November 2, 1961

While Norick was in Florida as a guest of the Air Force, the council took advantage of the situation and named five members of their own choosing.

November 21, 1961

The Mayor and Madalynne flipped a switch to light the Christmas tree at 7 p.m. on Thanksgiving Day. Over 500 lights on the seven story tree lit up.

November 25, 1961

Oklahoma City's "Freedom" Christmas Parade attracted 60,000 to 80,000 people with Mayor Norick declaring Main Street in a special proclamation as "Freedom Avenue."

December 4, 1961

The first 1962 Oklahoma County license tag went to Norick with the number "1 – 1" on it.

December 6, 1961

The year of 1962 will be the "year of truth" according to the Oklahoma City Chamber of Commerce. Projects of special emphasis will be:

1. Adequate financing for city government.

2. Urban renewal and a master city plan.

3. Multi-purpose assembly center.
4. Expressways.
5. Industrial development.
6. Aviation facilities and airports.
7. Completion of the National Cowboy and Western Heritage Museum.
8. Completion of the water program.

December 12, 1961

Four councilmen walked out when the other four were prepared to vote pay raises for city employees. Mayor Norick, who could only vote to break ties, indicated he would support it. The remaining four voted for it and Norick did as well. A municipal judge later ruled it "a void act" because a quorum of city council was not present."

December 14, 1961

When a blue law with emergency effectiveness was passed during Christmas shopping season, an injunction was granted to maintain Sunday shopping until Jan. 29. Discount stores GEX, AMC, Spartan, Atlantic Mills and Factory Distributing challenged the validity of the emergency voted by the city council.

December 16, 1961

More than 3,500 youngsters showed up at the Mayor's Christmas Party in the Municipal Auditorium.

December 19, 1961

Annexation of 4,100 acres on the northwest side occurred. Council also voted to acquire a tape recorder to record council meetings. When one councilman objected by saying

that the secretary already records the meeting on paper, Mayor Norick responded, "Yes, she takes down everything important that is said – and sometimes she isn't very busy." Meaning, sometimes there's not much being said that's important.

January 9, 1962

In far southeast Oklahoma City 160 acres were annexed.

January 17, 1962

Photos showed the new baseball stadium under construction by Manhattan Construction Company.

January 23, 1962

A major expansion and improvement program for the state fairgrounds was announced to be completed by 1970.

January 30, 1962

Ray Martin, Ward 2 councilman, took another opportunity to throw barbs at the tape recorder idea. He complained how one person listened to the tapes from a previous meeting and misunderstood something that was said. When informed that a log was kept of who listened to them and that only one councilman and the council secretary had listened to any tapes, he changed subjects. Martin wanted to know why two important city employees had to operate the recorder. At that point, Ward 2 councilman William Ware shot back, "I understand through the city charter that councilmen are not supposed to interfere in personnel matters." Mayor Norick let out a laugh and added, "I'm happy to hear you say that. I've thought that for some time." That ended the tape recorder discussion.

March 6, 1962

It was announced that the new baseball stadium would be named the Oklahoma City All Sports Stadium.

March 21, 1962

Fifty-five square miles were annexed on the far west side of Oklahoma City that included Cimarron Field. That addition boosted Oklahoma City's total to 536 square miles.

March 26, 1962

District Court struck down the Sunday closing ordinance passed the previous November by the City Council.

March 28, 1962

The 1962 Junior Hospitality Follies were scheduled to be presented at the Municipal Auditorium on April 13th to fund University Hospital's image intensifier. Madalynne was there helping by bringing her dog to try out for a part.

March 29, 1962

When a group of Tulsa civic leaders flew to Oklahoma City, they were given a red carpet tour by Mayor Norick. According to the Tulsa Tribune, "They toured the mushrooming Federal Aviation Center, the Aero Commander factory and the new Wiley Post airport where the group was briefed on the master plans for each of the city's airports. Returning to the downtown area, the Tulsans were driven through the State Fair grounds and shown the new ballpark seating 10,000."

April 4, 1962

"I'm glad to find out that I'm important," Mayor Norick joked when the city attorney issued a new ruling. The municipal counselor's office determined that the Oklahoma City charter and state laws on zoning by municipalities required the mayor's vote to be included. The mayor has previously only voted when there was a tie in the council. With two council members out of town, eleven ordinances were voted on with all seven votes, including Norick's, as for the ordinances. This was a precedent-setting vote.

April 7, 1962

Another 71 square miles were annexed in far northwest and southwest Oklahoma City.

April 11, 1962

The Mayor's Committee for City Beautification was formed with 50 volunteer citizens including Madalynne Norick. Several goals were set including anti-litter, flower and garden clubs, civic and service clubs.

April 20, 1962

A sold-out ballpark welcomed baseball back to Oklahoma City as the 89ers played in the new stadium. Shirt-sleeved Jim Norick tossed the first ball in the park on the evening of April 19, 1962.

April 26, 1962

Oklahoma City extended its limits into a sixth county, annexing 320 acres in Pottawatomie County.

May 10, 1962

Mayor Norick broke ground with Governor Edmondson for the new Southwest turnpike to Lawton.

May 22, 1962

Eleven square miles northeast of Oklahoma City were annexed.

June 5, 1962

While Norick was out of town, Ward 4 councilman Harold Johnson as acting Mayor appointed Paul Nunn to the city planning commission. Upon returning, Norick questioned the propriety of Nunn's appointment. Referring to Johnson's and the council's actions, Norick asked, "Do you want me to leave? If you guys have any cute little things (just like this appointment) you want to do, I'll leave before we adjourn."

June 12, 1962

Right-of-way for about half of the proposed Crosstown Expressway would be available to the State Highway Department within 90 days.

June 23, 1962

Jim Roederer, President of the city All Sports Association called for Oklahoma City to raise funds this year for a huge, multi-purpose assembly center. He said plans suggest it be built downtown. Previously it was suggested to the council that it be located on the fairgrounds.

July 4, 1962

The headline read, "$7.5 Million Sports Convention Project Proposed for City." The state fair board proposed an all-sports arena at the fairgrounds, a downtown convention hall and complete renovation of Municipal Auditorium into a music hall. The arena would seat 7,500 and cost approximately $2 million. The Municipal Auditorium renovation was estimated at $500,000. Stanley Draper said, "We feel the three facilities are absolutely necessary. There is no doubt there is a great need for them. One supports the other."

August 1, 1962

Belle Isle library contracts will be let in October. The library would be built on the corner of N. Villa and the Northwest Highway.

August 1, 1962

Mayor Norick reappointed Dr. F.D. Moon to the Oklahoma City Urban Renewal Authority after his original one-year term had expired.

August 2, 1962

On August 11, Tinker would welcome Maj. Leroy Gordon Cooper, one of the Original 7 Mercury astronauts born in Shawnee. Mayor Norick, Sen. Monroney and Gov. Edmondson would be on hand to welcome him.

September 9, 1962

A city-wide bus strike neared as over 100 members of the Amalgamated Association of Street, Electric Railway, and Motor Coach employees of America, Div. 993 voted for a September 9 strike.

September 6, 1962

When Mayor Norick refused to sign an ordinance passed by the city council majority changing ward boundary lines, the Oklahoma City Times editorial read, "The public relations of the council wasn't helped by its ignoring a citizens committee named by Mayor Norick to study proposed changes. It has been evident that the council majority and the mayor miss no opportunity to gig each other. But this time the calculated rebuke to the mayor may have nettled a lot of citizens who thought that by this time the council might be wise to let someone else have a hand at what they had botched."

September 7, 1962

Norick wanted to delay the redistricting until a citizen's committee had completed its report. Municipal Counselor Roy Semtner was asked by Ward 1 councilman Harry Bell if the mayor had the power to veto ordinances adopted by the city council. As Semtner answered, "No," the mayor banged the gavel to end the meeting, showing his power. Once a change has been made, another change could not be made until there is a 25% variance in registered voters between wards.

October 4, 1962

Work began to change the council chamber from groups of four at opposite sides of the room to a semicircular arrangement of desks, as well as a new sound system. The first meeting at the new "horseshoe" was October 9, 1962.

October 7, 1962

In a letter to 2,200 Oklahoma City area employers on the eve of National Employ the Handicapped Week, Mayor Norick asked for increased opportunities to hire handicapped persons. It marked the first time the city has made an effort to encourage this.

October 17, 1962

William Ware, Ward 2, lectured

Norick about the necessity for the mayor to consult councilmen on appointments. "People with integrity I will listen to," was the Mayor's response. Harry Bell, Ward 1, jumped in and said, "When I first came on council we were pretty good friends." Norick replied, "That was before you turned."

October 25, 1962

Mayor Norick was on hand as the very first Civil Defense supplies were loaded into the state's first Civil Defense shelter in the Hightower Building.

October 20, 1962

A 40 foot high Nike Hercules missile replica monument was presented to Mayor Norick as a gift to Oklahoma City from the U.S. Army Air Defense Command. It was placed on the east side of the courthouse.

October 30, 1962

Norick was authorized to appoint members of a new 5-member port authority in anticipation of Senator Robert S. Kerr's Red River navigation project when the Canadian River is made navigable.

November 1, 1962

The first Oklahoma City Urban Renewal action was taken when approval of the first designated "blight areas" was made by council.

November 4, 1962

At 12:01 a.m. direct long-distance dialing became a reality in Oklahoma City. The first call was made by Mayor and Mrs. Norick. The instructions were: dial "1" to indicate it is a direct dial call, then the area code of the city you are calling, then the phone number.

November 6, 1962

The five new members of the Oklahoma City Port Authority were named by Norick.. They were: William Cain (Cain's Coffee), Orville Mosier (American Airlines), C.A. Vose (1st National Bank), Leo Smith (Capitol Hill Savings and Loan), and Harvey Everest (Liberty National Bank).

November 22, 1962

Leroy Hansen, city civil defense director, offered the mayor and city councilmen two-way radios for communications in case of a disaster.

November 22, 1962

Work on the Crosstown Expressway begins in December by clearing buildings as the first step.

November 27, 1962

A $47.4 million bond issue passed on Nov. 27th providing for a new parallel runway at the airport and a new terminal building. Also included will be a new arena to be built at the State Fairgrounds.

November 28, 1962

After the City Council appointed a committee to study city finances, they chose to move ahead before the committee reported. The committee members became upset and resigned. At this, Mayor Norick appointed his own committee to study ways to help the city tackle the problem of adequate financing. The mayor said

that he would not ask for council approval because of previous rebuffs on his appointments. It would be an unofficial group, but with influential business leaders on-board, it would carry some weight with the community. *The Daily Oklahoman* referred to this action as the "opening gun in next spring's city elections."

December 8, 1962

The first Urban Renewal project funding application was authorized. The area would be in the vicinity of the University Medical Center between Lincoln and Stonewall and N.E. 4th and N.E. Park.

December 12, 1962

Oklahoma City fallout shelters have 70,000 shelter spaces in 57 buildings. This is more than Washington, D.C.

December 18, 1962

Mayor Norick and Mrs. Walter Gray, president of the library board, broke ground for the new Belle Isle Library using a full-size bulldozer.

December 21, 1962

The total building permits of $73,555,997 set a record in 1961. However, after only 11 months in 1962, a new record was set at $73,712,523.

December 22, 1962

The Mayor's Christmas Party was held again at Municipal Auditorium. About 7,000 youngsters attended.

December 31, 1962

The city started the year of 1962 off with 483.112 square miles, ending with a total of 620.161 square miles.

January 1, 1963

Senator Robert S. Kerr dies of a heart attack.

January 14, 1963

Plans for the $15 million Shepherd Plaza shopping center were unveiled. The 54-acre shopping center would be constructed at N.W. 23rd and Villa.

And the battle for re-election begins...

April 9, 1963

James Norick's last day in office as Jack Wilkes is sworn in as mayor.

1967 TO 1971 MAYORAL TERM

April 11, 1967

James Norick is sworn in as mayor of Oklahoma City after a four year absence from the office.

September 16, 1967

Mrs. Ruth Norick (the Mayor's Mother), 70, was injured in a one-car accident on Will Rogers Turnpike. One passenger died and another was seriously injured. They had gone to Miami, Oklahoma to attend a meeting of china decorators.

September 25, 1967

The Tulsa Philharmonic Orchestra was scheduled to play in Oklahoma City at the State Fair of Oklahoma. Dwight Daily, conductor of the group, gave Mayor Norick some simple instruction on how to conduct the orchestra. Norick had agreed to be a mystery conductor. "I instructed him on the basics of conducting," Daily said before the performance. "I told him to do his best to get

the orchestra started." While waiting for his turn, Norick smiled and told newsmen that he acted like he didn't know anything about music. "Actually, I was a student conductor at Classen High School. I also went to Oklahoma Military Academy on a two-year music scholarship. I played the clarinet and the alto sax," Norick told the reporters. The number he was to conduct was "Stars and Stripes Forever." With all the aplomb of a John Phillip Sousa he tapped the music stand, held his arms in the air and began a flawless performance. After a standing ovation from the crowd, Daily told him that he had the last laugh.

September 27, 1967

The City Council approved a 330 foot tower and a new travel and transportation building at the State Fairgrounds.

December 7, 1967

Protesting the City Council's inaction on an "open housing" ordinance 250 to 300 protestors were to march through Capitol Hill on Dec. 11th. In calling for citizens to respect the rights of others, Norick said in a free and democratic society, "one of our most cherished privileges and rights is the expression of our opinions and beliefs in a peaceful and open manner. This right of free expression is guaranteed to us by our constitution as well as by every tradition that we hold dear. On this coming Sunday, a group of our citizens are planning a parade through a portion of our community to express their belief and their ideas concerning an issue which is of vital concern to them and to our city." (The Open Housing Ordinance was passed in January, 1968)

December 20, 1967

Norick broke a 4-4 tie to begin work towards setting up a city turnpike authority. He had previously supported an Oklahoma County plan for city turnpikes. When that was struck down by the courts, he sought help from the State Highway Commission to get it through.

December 20, 1967

Sen. Mike Monroney was successful in getting $32.5 million released to Oklahoma City for urban renewal work downtown. "This is the big step we need to revitalize downtown," Norick said. City Manager Robert Oldland added, "It means we can expeditiously proceed with convention center site acquisition, clearance and plans for construction."

December 21, 1967

An artist's conception for the new convention center area showed possible additions of a major department store, hotel and motion picture theater.

February 6, 1968

Ron Norick was nominated for Outstanding Young Man of 1967 by the Oklahoma City Jaycees. He became President of the Jaycees on May 8, 1968 at the age of 26.

February 8, 1968

City garbage collectors were upset with working conditions and salaries. The biggest complaint was the shorthanded staff, causing them to be overworked.

February 10, 1968

Madalynne Norick's Red Cross work embarked on a new program seeking volunteers using the Greek word Ethelondis, meaning volunteer.

March 7, 1968

Work on Earlywine Park at Southwest 119th and Portland Avenue would begin next spring. A proposed 36-hole golf course is planned.

March 7, 1968

Madalynne is regent of the local Col. John Starke chapter of the Daughters of the American Revolution.

March 29, 1968

Funding was being gathered for a bridge to extend Shields Boulevard into downtown.

April 2, 1968

Oklahoma City Urban Renewal Authority purchased the land where the new Mummer's Theater will be built for $126,000.

April 2, 1968

Final plans were accepted by city council for the downtown convention center.

April 6, 1968

When Dr. Martin Luther King, Jr. was assassinated, Norick was in Washington, D.C. at a National League of Cities meeting. He issued a statement calling for "calm and orderly concern during this period of national tragedy." In a resolution by the mayor, he wrote: "Be it resolved that we join with all responsible Americans in using this tragic and sorrowful occasion to rededicate ourselves to the principles upon which our nation is built, and we pledge our full efforts toward safeguarding those rights, privileges and freedoms which are ours as Americans." Mayor and Mrs. Norick were pretty much confined to their hotel rooms during rioting in Washington, D.C. When Mayor Norick returned to Oklahoma City, Madalynne stayed on with friends to help the Red Cross.

April 25, 1968
City parks grew to 91 during 1967-68 financed by 1961-62 bonds. Plans called for 85 additional parks by 1985.

September 25, 1968
First contracts were readied for the successful bond issue passed in the Spring. Items include: sewer drains, traffic control, parks development, fire stations, zoo property and building, and airport improvements.

October 2, 1968
Jacksonville, Florida officially grabbed the title of largest city in land area from Oklahoma City.

October 2, 1968
Rowan and Martin and Phil Harris were in town for a charity golf tournament. They were given keys to the city by Mayor Norick.

October 8, 1968
The City Council established a turnpike trust with a 5 to 4 vote, Mayor Norick casting the tie-breaker. The Oklahoma City Urban Expressway Authority will seek to construct an Oklahoma City Urban Expressway.

December 16, 1968
Approval of 75,000 acre feet of water rights on McGee Creek Reservoir and 100,000 acre feet from Kiamichi River will provide water for Oklahoma City in years to come. McGee Creek is 30 miles northeast of the Atoka Reservoir. Frank Taylor, Water Utilities Director, said, "If the Atoka Reservoir had not been completed in 1964, we would be rationing water now in Oklahoma City."

December 31, 1968
Governor Bartlett wants the city to tie it's urban toll road in with the Tulsa to Stillwater turnpike being planned by the State turnpike authority. Mayor Norick said their eagerness to tie in with the Oklahoma City road must mean it could be lucrative. "If it's that good, Oklahoma City ought to keep it," he added.

January 11, 1969
Mayor Norick led a group of businessmen to Peru, investigating business partnerships in the South American country.

January 16, 1969
Norick appointed Roosevelt Turner as Director of the Mayor's Action for Youth Opportunities. It's designed to help disadvantaged youth 16 to 21 through job development, recreation, education and culture. The mayor is Executive Director of the program.

January 16, 1969
County Commissioners balked at setting up a joint turnpike authority with the city. They wanted more support than a tie-breaker vote gave them. Further action would wait

until new council members take office in the Spring. The Citizens panel recommended that the state build it.

May 17, 1969

Norick nominates Cities Service Gas Company for a national award by Business Week Magazine for human resources development because of its "innovative" efforts to recruit minority employees. They worked with the urban League, Community Action Program, Opportunities Industrialization Center and Neighborhood Youth Corps.

June 24, 1969

Norick receives a letter from Vice President Spiro Agnew with an official invitation to attend the Apollo 11 moon launch.

July 9, 1969

Groundbreaking for the new convention center was held. The $23 million facility covers a four square block area. Two bond elections funded it: $5 million in 1962 and $18 million in 1968.

July 18, 1969

Concerning attending the moon launch, Norick called it, "A fantastic and thrilling accomplishment for all mankind. I was privileged to see the Apollo 11 launch from Cape Kennedy on Wednesday and I have followed this flight with more than casual interest. Not often that man can sit in his living room and watch history in the making."

July 18, 1969

Oklahoma City joined state and federal offices in calling for a holiday the day after the landing so everyone could watch the moonwalk.

July 21, 1969

"It can only be compared with Columbus' discovery of America," the Mayor declared.

July 30, 1969

The state's first historical district was accepted by the City Council covering an "L" shaped area from Northwest 22nd Street south to Northwest 13th Street and from Western Avenue to Robinson Avenue.

December 9, 1969

Originally called the Tivoli Gardens, land was purchased by the city council to develop shops, amphitheater and various cultural facilities in an area bounded by Sheridan, Robinson, Reno and Hudson Avenues. The price was $900,000.

December 9, 1969

Madalynne opened a specialty store in Shepherd Mall called "The Plum Tree" in the summer of 1968. She sold artistic and decorative items, maintaining a high quality of porcelain, china, glass, woodenware and imported novelties.

February 5, 1970

Mayor Norick met with President Nixon at a prayer breakfast in Washington, D.C.

March 4, 1970

The name "Myriad" was approved by the council for the new downtown convention center.

April 1970

Norick Brothers purchased land at Southwest 15th Street and Council Avenue for an additional Plant.

May 1970

Norick attended a Mayors Conference in Israel with twelve other United States mayors as guests of the Israeli government.

December 3, 1970

Norick attended the opening night of Mummer's Theater on Wednesday, December 2. The first performance was "A Man for All Seasons."

January 15, 1970

A special citizens committee proposed allowing the mayor the right to vote on all matters before the council.

This would be voted on by citizens in the March 16 election.

January 22, 1970

Jim Norick with Madalynne at his side, announced he would not seek a third term as mayor. Stating that he would devote as much time as possible to civic functions for the growth and betterment of Oklahoma City, Norick cited the demands of his private business as reason for stepping down. Citing several boards and authorities the mayor serves on, he mentioned the high demands on that person's time. Madalynne added, "I think we'll both miss it."

April 13, 1971

His last council meeting as Mayor.

APPENDIX C

RONALD NORICK TIME LINE
Beginning in 1987

April 14, 1987

Ron Norick is sworn in as mayor of Oklahoma City.

November 2, 1987

Mayor Ron Norick stepped in to get negotiations back underway between striking Oklahoma Symphony Orchestra musicians and management. Talks had been at a stalemate for almost a month.

December 16, 1987

Norick and the City Council attended the National League of Cities conference in Las Vegas, Nevada, attended by 5,000 municipal leaders from around the country.

Norick and leaders from other large cities discussed issues to present to presidential candidates.

January 25, 1988

Norick created the Mayor's Commission on Public Education to work with businesses and community organizations to promote education and improve the image of the Oklahoma City public schools.

March 2, 1988

Penn Square Mall celebrated its Grand Reopening with Mayor Norick, Oklahoma's first lady Shirley Bellmon, and Barry Switzer in attendance.

March 25, 1988

Norick cut the ribbon at the opening of the Crystal Bridge in the Myriad Gardens.

May 20, 1988

Norick joined six other U.S. cities in adopting the KidsPlace program. It is a chance for the children to tell the city what's right and what's wrong with it.

August 9, 1988

The Ninety-Nines opened their international headquarters at Will Rogers World Airport. Over 200 members from around the world helped celebrate the opening of this women's pilot organization.

January 10, 1989

Voters rejected a 1-cent sales tax, but there was some encouragement in the slim margin of defeat. Three recent tries had failed overwhelmingly, but this loss was by only 105 votes.

April 21, 1989

The Centennial Expressway was dedicated with speeches by Norick, Ed Martin, Neal McCaleb, George Nigh and Henry Bellmon. The $153 million road connected Interstate 35 to Interstate 44 and the Broadway Extension.

May 9, 1989

The City Council cancelled a $3.8 million loan agreement with owners of the Skirvin Hotel. They had failed to secure a letter of credit needed to complete the deal.

June 20, 1989

Voters approve a three-quarter-cent sales tax to help police and fire departments.

July 11, 1989

City Manager Terry Childers announced his resignation.

October 17, 1989

Paula Hearn begins her time as City Manager.

November 20, 1989

Norick announces the formation of an aerospace triangle from Tulsa to Wichita to Oklahoma City. This combined group sought to support regional expansion in the aviation industry.

March 3, 1990

AmCare became the primary provider for ambulance service in the metro area.

March 30, 1990

The "Mayor's Conference for Women in the 90s" was held as a forum to help women establish positive economic, social and political programs. The event was chaired by Terry Neese and Linda Richardson.

May 5, 1990

Oklahoma City University conferred an honorary doctorate of humane letters on Ron Norick.

September 20, 1990

Norick announced a $60 million holding facility for federal prisoners would be built at the airport.

November 9, 1990

The opening game of the Continental Basketball Association Oklahoma City Cavalry basketball team kicked off at the Myriad. Over 8,000 fans showed up to start the season.

December 13, 1990

Hearn announces she is leaving the City Manager's office to become director of the state Office of Public Affairs for Governor David Walters.

December 22, 1990

The 50th Annual Mayor's Christmas Party was held at the Myriad.

January 9, 1991

Norick announces plans to run for re-election.

February 26, 1991

Voters approve a county tax to help lure a United Airlines maintenance facility to Oklahoma City.

March 19, 1991

Norick is re-elected by more than 80 percent of the vote.

April 9, 1991

Norick is sworn in for a special three year term as mayor of Oklahoma City. In June of 1990, the citizens voted to change the city charter to elect the mayor in even numbered years and separate that office's election from the City Council elections. To accomplish this, the mayoral term beginning in 1991 would only be for three years to get it to an even numbered year in 1994.

October 23, 1991

Indianapolis wins United's maintenance facility.

November 4, 1992

Ice hockey returned to Oklahoma City after a 10-year absence when the Central Hockey League's Oklahoma City Blazers took the ice. Season

ticket holder Ron Norick was in attendance.

December 14, 1993

Metropolitan Area Projects (MAPS) passes 54 to 46 percent.

March 15, 1994

Norick received 70 percent of the vote in his bid for a third term as Mayor of Oklahoma City.

April 12, 1994

Norick begins his third and last term as mayor of Oklahoma City.

April 19, 1995

The Alfred P. Murrah Federal Building is destroyed by a truck bomb.

October 10, 1995

Groundbreaking for the new MAPS ballpark.

April 5, 1996

President Clinton traveled to Oklahoma City to meet with families and victims one year after the Murrah Building bombing.

April 9, 1997

NHL Commissioner Gary Bettman and the NHL Expansion Committee came to Oklahoma City to evaluate the community for a potential expansion team.

June 3, 1997

Groundbreaking for the new YMCA to replace the building destroyed by the Murrah building blast.

June 17, 1997

With a "too small TV market," the NHL passed on Oklahoma City.

July 1, 1997
The design for the Oklahoma City bombing memorial was selected. The committee selected the design unanimously on the first vote.

June, 1997
Construction begins on Myriad repairs and expansion, as well as the Bricktown Canal.

October 14, 1997
Glenn Deck was approved to become the next City Manager when Don Bown retires on Jan. 8, 1998.

October 29, 1997
Norick announces he would not seek a fourth term.

April 14, 1998
Ron Norick becomes a private citizen again as Kirk Humphries takes office as Mayor.

November 1998
Construction renovation begins on Civic Center.

Early 1999
Construction on the river damns and locks begin.

Spring 1999
Construction begins on the Arena.

July 2, 1999
Opening of the Bricktown Canal.

August 2000
Myriad work is completed and construction of the new library begins.

September 2001
Civic Center work is completed.

June 2002
The Arena opens.

Spring 2004
MAPS work on the river is completed.

August 17, 2004
The Ronald J. Norick Downtown library opens.

MAPS PROJECTS

STATE FAIR PARK

Renovations totaled $14 million. Improvements included a new livestock show facility, horse barns, arena renovation and several exhibition building changes. Completed by fall 1998, the engineers were Howell-Summers-Boyd and The Architectural Partnership. Contractors were Construction Building Specialities, Inc., L.F. Downey Construction Co., Inc., Lippert Brothers, Inc., Stephen & Associates Builders, Inc., T.J. Boismier, and J.L. Walker Construction Co.

Myriad Convention Center

Total cost was $63.1 million. More than 100,000 square feet was added including a new 25,000 square foot ballroom and integrated audio-visual equipment. Construction began in June 1997 and was completed in August 2000. The architect was Glover Smith Bode, Inc. General Contractor was Flintco Construction Co.

Bricktown Ballpark

Cost was $34.2 million. A two-level brick facility with natural grass field, seating capacity of 12,000 and luxury seats. Construction began in August 1996 and was completed in the spring 1998. Architect was

Architectural Design Group. General Contractor was Oscar J. Boldt Construction Co.

Bricktown Canal

Total cost was $23.1 million. Two different portions include a north section and a south section. Construction began summer 1997 and opened on July 2, 1999. Engineering by Johnson & Associates and Clowers Engineering. General Contractors were Oscar J. Boldt Construction Co. and Wyan Construction Co., Inc.

Civic Center Renovations

Cost was $52.4 million. A total interior renovation with a multistory atrium, balconies, box seats and suites. Construction began November 1998 and was completed September 2001. Architect was Richard R. Brown & Associates. General Contractor was Flintco Construction Co.

Sports Arena

Total cost was $87.7 million. A 20,000 seat, upholstered, padded seats, three levels and 581,000 square feet. Construction began spring 1998 and opened June 2002. Architect was The Benham Group. General contractor was Flintco Construction Co.

River and Dam System

Total cost was $51.8 million. Through the use of dams, a series of lakes were created along seven miles of the North Canadian River filling the riverway from bank to bank. Engineers were Triad Design Group, Espey, Huston & Associates Inc. General contractors were C-P Integrated Services Inc. and Wynn Construction Co.

Library Learning Center

Cost was $21.5 million. Replaces the 50-year-old downtown library with state-of-the-art information services and equipment, classroom space, traditional resources in a four level, 110,000 square foot facility. Architect was Beck Associates. General contractor was Buckner and Moore, Inc.

NORICK DOCUMENTS

THESE DOCUMENTS INCLUDE James Norick's two Oath of Office documents and the three Oath of Office documents from Ron Norick's terms.

Resolutions include the naming of the Jim Norick Arena, the Ronald J. Norick Downtown Library, and the ordinance naming Ron Norick Boulevard.

OATH OF OFFICE

STATE OF OKLAHOMA }
OKLAHOMA COUNTY } SS.

I, JAMES H. NORICK, do solemnly swear (or affirm)
that I will support, obey and defend the Constitution
of the United States, and the Constitution of the State
of Oklahoma, and the Charter of The City of Oklahoma City,
and will discharge the duties of my office with fidelity;
that I have not paid or contributed, either directly or
indirectly, any money or other valuable thing to procure
my election, except for necessary and proper expenses
authorized by law; that I have not knowingly violated
any election law of the State, or procured it to be done
by others in my behalf; that I will not knowingly receive,
directly or indirectly, any money or other valuable thing
for the performance or non-performance of any act or duty
pertaining to my office other than the compensation
allowed by law, and I further swear (or affirm) that I
will not receive, use, or travel upon any free pass or
on free transportation during my term of office.

James H. Norick
James H. Norick

Subscribed and sworn to before me this 14th day
of April, 1959.

Fred Daugherty

Official Title
Seventh Judicial District
State of Oklahoma,

OATH OF OFFICE

I, ...James H. Norick, Mayor of The City of Oklahoma City,....................
do solemnly swear (or affirm) that I will support, obey, and defend the Constitution of the United States, and the Constitution of the State of Oklahoma and will discharge the duties of my office with fidelity; that I have not paid, or contributed, either, directly or indirectly, and money or other valuable thing, to procure my nomination or election (or appointment), except for necessary and proper expenses expressly authorized by law; that I have not, knowingly, violated any election law of the State, or procured it to be done by others in my behalf; that I will not, knowingly, receive, directly or indirectly, any money or other valuable thing, for the performance or non-performance of any act or duty pertaining to my office, other than the compensation allowed by law, and I further swear (or affirm) that I will not receive, use or travel upon any free pass or on free transportation during my term of office.

James H. Norick
James H. Norick   Principal

Subscribed and sworn to before me this ....11....day of ....April........ 19 67

[signature]
Notary Public

My commission expires: ....
municipal Counselor

Oath Of Office

I, _____RONALD J. NORICK_____, do solemnly swear (or affirm) that I will support, obey, and defend the Constitution of the United States, and the Constitution of the State of Oklahoma, and will discharge the duties of my office with fidelity; that I have not paid, or contributed either directly or indirectly, any money or other valuable thing, to procure my nomination or election (or appointment), except for necessary and proper expenses expressly authorized by law; that I have not knowingly violated any election law of the State, or procured it to be done by others in my behalf; that I will not knowingly receive, directly or indirectly, any money or other valuable thing, for the performance or non-performance of any act or duty pertaining to my office, other than the compensation allowed by law, and I further swear (or affirm) that I will not receive, use or travel upon any free pass or on free transportation during my term of office.

[signature]
(signature of person sworn)

Subscribed and sworn to before me

this _14th_ day of _April_ A.D., 19 87

[signature]
Notary Public or other officer authorized
to administer oaths or affirmations

(Seal)

R E S O L U T I O N

A RESOLUTION OF COMMENDATION AND COMMEMORATION

WHEREAS, James H. Norick has untiringly devoted himself to the development of creative and effective government for The Citizens of The City of Oklahoma City; and

WHEREAS, during his twelve years of service with The City of Oklahoma City, four years as councilman and eight years as its Mayor, James H. Norick lead The City of Oklahoma City to unprecedented heights of industrial growth and economic expansion; and

WHEREAS, James H. Norick's devotion and dedication to sports events in The City of Oklahoma City, to-wit: promotion of the Central Hockey League and the Oklahoma City Blazers, has made this City one of the great sports cities in the Southwest United States; and

WHEREAS, it is the desire of the Citizens and the Council of The City of Oklahoma City to commend James H. Norick for his devotion to The City of Oklahoma City and express their gratitude to him for his effectiveness as a community leader.

NOW, THEREFORE, BE IT RESOLVED by the Council of The City of Oklahoma City that the Sports Arena located at the Oklahoma City Fairgrounds be hereinafter denoted and named the

"JIM NORICK ARENA"

ADOPTED by the Council and APPROVED by the Mayor of The City of Oklahoma City this 13th day of April, 1971.

—————————————————
M A Y O R

ATTEST:

OATH OF OFFICE

I, RONALD J. NORICK, do solemnly swear (or affirm) that I will support, obey, and defend the Constitution of the United States, and the Constitution of the State of Oklahoma, and that I will not, knowingly, receive, directly or indirectly, any money or other valuable thing, for the performance or nonperformance of any act or duty pertaining to my office, other than the compensation allowed by law; I further swear (or affirm) that I will faithfully discharge my duties as Mayor of The City of Oklahoma City to the best of my ability.

_____
RONALD J. NORICK

This instrument was acknowledged before me on the 12th day of April, 1994, by Ronald J. Norick.

(SEAL)

_____
Notary Public, or other officer
authorized to administer oaths
or affirmations

Art. 15 § 1 Okla. Const.

The City of Oklahoma City
Office of the Mayor
Resolution

WHEREAS, Ronald J. Norick served as Mayor of the City of Oklahoma City from April 14, 1987, to April 14, 1998, being one of only three Mayors elected to serve three consecutive terms of office; and

WHEREAS, Ronald J. Norick recognized the need to lead Oklahoma City from the economic doldrums and create a more vibrant, active city, and he worked with civic and community leaders to develop the Metropolitan Area Projects (MAPS) program to construct or renovate eight public facilities and provide a new downtown transportation system; and

WHEREAS, Ronald J. Norick's leadership was key to winning voter approval in December 1993, of the five-year, limited purpose sales tax to fund the MAPS projects which were the Bricktown Ballpark, State Fair Park renovations, Bricktown Canal, Civic Center Renovation, Library-Learning Center, Convention Center renovation and expansion, North Canadian River dams and lakes, a new downtown Arena, and the Transportation link; and

WHEREAS, Ronald J. Norick's promise that MAPS would lead to economic redevelopment has been fulfilled, as the completion of six of the MAPS facilities has resulted in the revitalization of our downtown, with over $1 billion of public investment having been completed or planned, and Oklahoma City is receiving national attention as a great place to live, to visit, and to do business; and

WHEREAS, Ronald J. Norick's commitment to this City and its citizens continues to be expressed in many areas of public service including his strong support of programs for education and youth and his service as Chairman of the Oklahoma City Riverfront Redevelopment Authority; and

WHEREAS, the MAPS Library and Learning Center building at Park Avenue and Hudson Avenue will open in 2004, and it is the desire of the City Council to permanently recognize the visionary leadership and dedicated service of Ronald J. Norick; and

WHEREAS, the City Council has the right to name the new building and discussions have been held with the Metropolitan Library Commission, and the members of the Commission are in agreement with the proposed name.

NOW, THEREFORE, BE IT RESOLVED by the Vice Mayor and Council of the City of Oklahoma City that the new library be called the "Ronald J. Norick Downtown Library," and providing said name be used in the monumental sign for the building and in all legal documents.

ADOPTED by the Council and **SIGNED** by the Vice Mayor this ___30th___ day of ___December___, 2003.

_____
VICE MAYOR

ATTEST:

_____
City Clerk

Reviewed for Form and Legality this ___ day of ___December___, 2003.

_____
Assistant Municipal Counselor

SN-009   (Published in The Journal Record _June 17_, 19 _98_)

ORDINANCE NO. _21,065_

AN ORDINANCE PROVIDING THAT ROBINSON AVENUE, BETWEEN RENO AVENUE AND SHERIDAN AVENUE, BE HEREAFTER DESIGNATED AS RON NORICK BOULEVARD, AND PROVIDING FOR AN EMERGENCY.

EMERGENCY ORDINANCE

BE IT ORDAINED BY THE COUNCIL OF THE CITY OF OKLAHOMA CITY:

SECTION 1. That Robinson Avenue, between Reno Avenue and Sheridan Avenue, as shown in the final plat of Oklahoma City Original, is hereby designated as Ron Norick Boulevard.

SECTION 2. (EMERGENCY) WHEREAS, it being immediately necessary for the preservation of the peace, health, safety, and public good of Oklahoma City and the inhabitants thereof that the provisions of this Ordinance be put into full force and effect, an emergency is hereby declared to exist by reason whereof this Ordinance shall take effect and be in full force immediately upon and after it adoption by the Council of The City of Oklahoma City as provided by law.

INTRODUCED AND CONSIDERED in open meeting of the Council of The City of Oklahoma City on this 26th day of May, 1998.

PASSED by the Council of The City of Oklahoma City on this ___16___ day of _____June_____, 1998.

SIGNED by the Mayor of The City of Oklahoma City on this ___16___ day of _____June_____, 1998.

_____
MAYOR

ATTEST:

BIBLIOGRAPHY

BOOKS:

Burke, Bob with Joan Gilmore, *Old Man River, the Life of Ray Ackerman,* Oklahoma Heritage Association, Oklahoma City, OK, 2002.

Horrow, Rick with Larry Bloom, *When the Game is on the Line,* Perseus Publishing, Cambridge, MA, 2003.

Smallwood, James M., *Urban Builder: Life and Times of Stanley Draper,* University of Oklahoma Press, Norman, OK, 1977.

Meredith, Howard and Mary Ellen Meredith, *Mr. Oklahoma History: The Life of George H. Shirk,* Western Heritage Books, Inc., 1982.

NEWSPAPER:

The Daily Oklahoman.
Oklahoma City Times.
Black Dispatch.
North Star.

TAPES:

Living Legends Oral History Collection, Research Division, Oklahoma Historical Society.

MANUSCRIPT ITEMS:

Norick Collection, Research Division, Oklahoma Historical Society.

PERIODICALS:

Towntalk, a publication of the Oklahoma Municipal Contractors Association.

ENDNOTES

Chapter I

1. Norick, George Alonzo, *Important and Interesting Events of My Career*, (an unpublished manuscript in James Norick's possession), 1950, p. 3.
2. Interview with Henry Norick, June 15, 1971, Living Legends Oral History Series, Research Division, Oklahoma Historical Society.
3. Norick, George Alonzo, Ibid., p. 29-30.
4. *The Daily Oklahoman*, February 23, 1967.
5. Norick, George Alonzo, Ibid., p. 31.
6. Living Legends, Henry Norick, Ibid.
7. Norick, George Alonzo, Ibid., p. 32-33.
8. Norick, George Alonzo, Ibid., p. 36.
9. Interview with Roy Evans, June 25, 1970, Living Legends Oral History Collection, Research Division, Oklahoma Historical Society.
10. Interview with Jim and Madalynne Norick, June 15, 1971, Living Legends Oral History Collection, Research Division, Oklahoma Historical Society.
11. Living Legends, Jim and Madalynne Norick, Ibid.
12. Interview with James Norick by author, October 3, 2002.
13. Ibid.

Chapter II

1. James and Madalynne Norick, Living Legends Oral History Collection, Oklahoma Historical Society, June 15, 1971.
2. Ibid.
3. Ibid.
4. Ibid.
5. Ibid.
6. *The Daily Oklahoman*, March 19, 1951.
7. Ibid., Living Legends.
8. *The Daily Oklahoman*, March 19, 1951.
9. Ibid., March 23, 1951.
10. *Oklahoma City Times*, March 23, 1951.
11. *The Daily Oklahoman*, March 23, 1951.
12. Ibid., April 4, 1951.
13. Script from Bob Eastman Commentary, Norick Collection, Research Division, Oklahoma Historical Society.
14. John Jarman letter, Norick Collection, Research Division, Oklahoma Historical Society.
15. *The Daily Oklahoman*, April 4, 1951.

CHAPTER III

1. *The Daily Oklahoman*, June 28, 1951.
2. *The Daily Oklahoman*, Sept. 18, 1951.
3. *The Daily Oklahoman*, Jan. 13-20, 1952.
4. *The Daily Oklahoman*, June 4, 1952.
5. *The Daily Oklahoman*, July 24, 1952.
6. *The Daily Oklahoman*, June 29, 1954.
7. Letter from John Jarman, Feb. 23, 1955, James Norick Collection, Research Division, Oklahoma Historical Society.

CHAPTER IV

1. *The Daily Oklahoman*, July 27, 1955.
2. *The Daily Oklahoman*, June 29, 1956.
3. *The Daily Oklahoman*, Jan. 12, 1957.
4. *The Daily Oklahoman*, Jan. 28, 1959.
5. *Oklahoma City Times*, March 18, 1959.
6. *The Daily Oklahoman*, March 23, 1959.
7. Ibid.
8. *The Daily Oklahoman*, April 7, 1959.
9. *The Daily Oklahoman*, April 8, 1959.

CHAPTER V

1. *The Daily Oklahoman*, April 8, 1959.
2. *The Daily Oklahoman*, October 9, 1959.
3. *Oklahoma City Times*, October 7, 1959
4. *Oklahoma City Times*, October 10, 1959.
5. *The Daily Oklahoman*, October 15, 1959.
6. *Oklahoma City Times*, October 15, 1959.
7. *Oklahoma City Times*, December 26, 1959.
8. *The Daily Oklahoman*, August 24, 1960.
9. *Oklahoma City Times*, September 6, 1960.
10. *The Daily Oklahoman*, September 10, 1960.
11. *Oklahoma City Times*, October 31, 1961.
12. *Oklahoma City Times*, March 1, 1960.

CHAPTER VI

1. Southwest Water Works Journal, Oct. 1967, P. 31-39.
2. *Oklahoma City Times*, May 5, 1960.
3. *Oklahoma City Times*, Oct. 30, 1959.
4. *Oklahoma City Times*, Dec. 8, 1959.
5. *Oklahoma City Times*, April 12, 1960.
6. *Oklahoma City Advertiser*, April 14, 1960.
7. *Oklahoma City Times*, April 14, 1960.
8. *NorthStar*, April 21, 1960.
9. *Oklahoma City Times*, Aug. 5, 1960.
10. *The Daily Oklahoman*, Aug. 16, 1960.
11. *The Daily Oklahoman*, Sept. 13, 1960.
12. *The Daily Oklahoman*, Dec. 17, 1960.
13. *The Daily Oklahoman*, Jan. 18, 1961.
14. *The Daily Oklahoman*, May 10, 1961.
15. *Ada News*, Aug. 3, 1961.
16. *The Daily Oklahoman*, Oct. 12, 1961.

17. *Oklahoma City Times*, March 14, 1962.
18. *Oklahoma City Times*, July 27, 1962.
19. *The Daily Oklahoman*, July 28, 1962.
20. *The Daily Oklahoman*, July 30, 1962.
21. *The Daily Oklahoman*, Dec. 26, 1962.
22. *The Daily Oklahoman*, July 31, 1964.
23. *Advertiser*, June 22, 1967.
24. *Oklahoma City Times*, July 12, 1967.

CHAPTER VII
1. *Oklahoma City Times*, Jan. 22, 1963.
2. *The Advertiser*, March 3, 1963.
3. *The Advertiser*, Feb. 7, 1963
4. *Oklahoma City Times*, Jan. 31, 1963.
5. *Black Dispatch*, Feb. 15, 1963.
6. *The Daily Oklahoman*, Feb. 20, 1963.
7. *Capitol Hill Beacon*, Feb. 24, 1963.
8. *The Daily Oklahoman*, Feb. 24, 1963.

9. *The Daily Oklahoman*, Feb. 20, 1963.
10. *The Daily Oklahoman*, March 1, 1963.
11. *North Star*, March 7, 1963.
12. *The Daily Oklahoman*, March 9, 1963.
13. *Oklahoma City Times*, March 9, 1963.
14. *The Daily Oklahoman*, March 10, 1963.
15. *Oklahoma City Times*, March 11, 1963.
16. *Oklahoma City Times*, March 13, 1963.
17. *The Daily Oklahoman*, March 16, 1963.
18. *Oklahoma City Times*, March 20, 1963.
19. Ibid.

CHAPTER VIII
1. *Oklahoma City Times*, March 17, 1964.
2. "Mr. Oklahoma History, The Life of George H. Shirk," by Howard and Mary Ellen Meredith, Oklahoma Heritage Association, 1982.
3. *Oklahoma City Times*, March 12, 1964.

4. *The Daily Oklahoman*, March 5, 1964.
5. *Oklahoma City Times*, March 9, 1964.
6. *The Daily Oklahoman*, Sept. 24, 1964.
7. *The Daily Oklahoman*, Dec. 18, 1964.
8. *The Daily Oklahoman*, Feb. 5, 1965.
9. *The Daily Oklahoman*, Jan. 1, 1967.
10. *Oklahoma Journal*, March 2, 1967.
11. *Oklahoma Journal*, March 6, 1967.
12. *Oklahoma Journal*, March 15, 1967.
13. *Oklahoma Journal*, March 29, 1967.
14. *Oklahoma City Times*, March 22, 1967.
15. *The Daily Oklahoman*, March 26, 1967.
16. *Oklahoma City Times*, March 29, 1967.
17. *Oklahoma Journal*, March 31, 1967.
18. *Oklahoma City Times*, April 1, 1967.
19. *Oklahoma City Times*, April 5, 1967.

20. *The Daily Oklahoman*, April 5, 1967.
21. *Oklahoma Journal*, April 12, 1967.
22. *The Daily Oklahoman*, April 18, 1967.
23. *Oklahoma Journal*, May 20, 1967.
24. *Oklahoma City Times*, May 19, 1967.
25. *The Daily Oklahoman*, May 30, 1967.
26. *Oklahoma City Times*, June 6, 1967.
27. *Oklahoma City Times*, June 21, 1967.
28. *Oklahoma Journal*, June 15, 1967.
29. *The Daily Oklahoman*, July 14, 1967.
30. *Oklahoma City Times*, July 26, 1967.
31. *The Daily Oklahoman*, July 29, 1967.

CHAPTER IX
1. *Oklahoma City Times*, Aug. 4, 1969.
2. *The Daily Oklahoman*, Aug. 5, 1969.
3. Oklahoma City Times, Aug. 14, 1969.

4. *The Daily Oklahoman*, Aug. 5, 1969.
5. *Oklahoma City Times*, Aug. 19, 1969.
6. *Oklahoma Journal*, Aug. 20, 1969.
7. *The Daily Oklahoman*, Aug. 21, 1969.
8. *The Daily Oklahoman*, Aug. 22, 1969.
9. *Oklahoma Journal*, Aug. 28, 1969.
10. *Oklahoma Journal*, Sept. 4, 1969.
11. *Oklahoma City Times*, Sept. 3, 1969.
12. *The Daily Oklahoman*, Sept. 17, 1969.
13. *Oklahoma Journal*, Sept. 23, 1969.
14. *The Daily Oklahoman*, Sept. 23, 1969.
15. *The Daily Oklahoman*, Oct. 22, 1969.
16. *Oklahoma City Times*, Oct. 24, 1969.
17. Ibid.
18. *The Daily Oklahoman*, Oct. 31, 1969.
19. *Oklahoma Journal*, Oct. 29, 1969.
20. *The Daily Oklahoman*, Oct. 31, 1969.

21. *Oklahoma City Times*, Oct. 31, 1969.
22. *Oklahoma Journal*, Oct. 25, 1969.
23. *The Daily Oklahoman*, Nov. 1, 1969.
24. *Oklahoma City Times*, Oct. 30, 1969.
25. *Oklahoma Journal*, Nov. 3, 1969.
26. *The Daily Oklahoman*, Nov. 7, 1969.
27. Ibid.

CHAPTER X
1. Copy of Press Release, in possession of James Norick, January 22, 1971.

CHAPTER XI
1. Ron Norick interview with author, Norick Investment Co., Oklahoma City, Ok, May 2, 2000.
2. Ibid.
3. Ibid.
4. Ibid.
5. Ibid.
6. Ibid.
7. Ibid.
8. Ron Norick interview with author, Norick Investments, Oklahoma City, Ok, July 6, 2000.
9. Ibid.
10. Ibid.

11. Ibid.
12. Ibid.
13. Ibid.

CHAPTER XII
1. Ron Norick interview with author, Norick Investments, Oklahoma City, OK, July 6, 2000.
2. Ibid.
3. Ibid.
4. Ibid.
5. Ibid.
6. Ibid.
7. Ibid.
8. Ibid.

CHAPTER XIII
1. *Daily Oklahoman,* April 15, 1987.
2. *Daily Oklahoman,* April 15, 1987.
3. *Daily Oklahoman,* April 26, 1987.
4. *Daily Oklahoman,* June 12, 1987.
5. *Daily Oklahoman,* March 27, 1988.
6. *Daily Oklahoman,* Sept. 30, 1988.
7. Ibid., Dec. 9, 1988.
8. Ibid., Jan. 8, 1989.
9. Ibid., June 21, 1989.
10. *Daily Oklahoman,* March 21, 1989.
11. Ibid., March 24, 1989.
12. Ibid., June 8, 1989.
13. Ibid., March 22, 1989.
14. Ibid., April 26, 1989.

15. Ibid., May 6, 1989.
16. Ibid., Feb. 18, 1990.
17. Ibid., Feb. 22, 1990.
18. Ibid., March 19, 1990.

CHAPTER XIV
1. Ron Norick interview with author, Norick Investments, Oklahoma City, OK, Aug. 17, 2000.
2. Ibid.
3. *Daily Oklahoman,* Jan. 24, 1991.
4. Ibid., Jan. 9, 1991.
5. Ibid., Jan. 15, 1991.
6 .Ibid., Feb. 20, 1991.
7. Ibid., Feb. 24, 1991.
8. Ibid., Feb. 27, 1991.
9. Ibid., Oct. 24, 1991.
10. Ibid, Norick interview, Aug. 17, 2000.
11. *Daily Oklahoman,* Sept. 7, 1988.
12. Ibid., Norick interview, Aug. 17, 2000.
13. Don Bown telephone interview with author, July 19, 2004.
14. Horrow, Rick with Larry Bloom, *When the Game is on the Line,* Perseus Publishing, Cambridge, MA, 2003.
15. *Daily Oklahoman,* Nov. 17, 2003.

16. Jim Bruza interview with author, FSB, Oklahoma City, OK, January 9, 2004.
17. *Daily Oklahoman,* July 4, 2004.
18. *Towntalk,* Nov./Dec. 2003, p. 15.

CHAPTER XV
1. Ron Norick interview with author, Norick Investments, Oklahoma City, OK, Aug. 17, 2000.
2. Ibid.
3. *Daily Oklahoman,* April 20, 1995.
4. Interview by author, Aug. 17, 2000.
5. Ibid.
6. Mary Fallin interview by author, Lt. Governor's office, State Capitol, Jan. 9, 2004.
7. Frank Keating interview by author, Governor's office, State Capitol, Aug. 14, 2000.
8. Gary Marrs telephone interview by author, July 19, 2004.
9. Mark Schwartz telephone interview by author, July 19, 2004.
10. Don Bown telephone interview by author, July 19, 2004.

CHAPTER XVI
1. *Daily Oklahoman,* Jan. 1, 1996.
2. Ibid.
3. Ibid, Feb. 7, 1996.
4. Ibid., Feb. 15, 1996
5. Ibid., Feb. 18, 1996.
6. Ibid., April 19, 1996.
7. Ibid., July 19, 1996.
8. Ibid., Sept. 10, 1996.
9. Ibid., Sept. 12, 1996.
10. Ibid., Nov. 20, 1996.
11. Ibid., Feb. 20, 1997.
12. Ibid., April 10, 1997.
13. Ibid., June 3, 1997.
14. Ibid., July 2, 1997.
15. Ibid., Oct. 5, 1997.
16. Ibid., Oct. 29, 1997.
17. Ibid., Sept. 8, 1997.

Epilogue
1. *The Daily Oklahoman,* Aug. 17, 2004.
2. Ibid., March 21, 2001.
3. Ibid., March 26, 2001
4. Ibid., Dec. 23, 1998.
5. Ibid., April 13, 1998.

INDEX

A

Abernathy, Ralph 127, 129, 131
Ackerman, Ray 107-111, 181
ACOG 118, 141
Adopt-a-Pothole 176
ADP 156
Agnew, Spiro 289
All Sports Stadium 199, 203, 282
AMC 281
AmCare 187, 292
American Airlines 173, 183-184, 186, 193
American Institute of Architects 241
Amis Construction 90
Anthony, Nancy 200
"Apollo 11" 289
Arena 203, 205, 207, 251, 256, 260, 294-295
ATF 223
Atlantic Mills 278, 281
Atoka Reservoir 81-85, 87, 89-91, 260, 288
Automobile Alley 256

B

Baker, Robert W. 186
Ballpark 203, 205, 211, 253-254, 256

Barnes, Joe B. 202
Bartlett, Dewey 130, 132-133, 288
Baseball 278-282
Basketball 292
Bee, Ed 194
Bell, Harry 284
Bellmon, Henry 175-176, 184, 186-187, 292
Bellmon, Shirley 291
Benecke, Tex 28, 31
Bennett, Clayton I. 202, 250
Bethany, OK 41
Bettman, Gary 252
Bishop, Bill 167
Blackburn, Debbie 187
Bledsoe, Larry 271
Boldt Construction 245
Bowlarena 143, 149
Bown, Don 8, 202, 234, 255
Bricktown 205, 212, 243, 246
Bricktown Merchants Association 239
Bruza, Jim 8, 204-205, 218
Buchanan, Buck 202
Bull, Linda 8
Bulla, Merton 62-63, 162

Burba, Charles 62-63, 66, 71, 162
Burke, Andy 237
Burke, Bob 6, 8
Burnell, Bud 146
Burton, Joe 242
Bush, George H.W. 184

C

Campbell, Gini 6, 8
Canal 205, 207, 211, 214, 248-249, 256, 294-295
Carey, Jackie 181, 183, 186, 189, 201, 206, 212
Centennial Expressway 186, 292
Central National Bank 266
Chang, Hong-Yih 267
Childers, Terry 170, 175, 182-183, 186, 292
"Cimarron" 278
Cimarron Field 282
Cisneros, Henry 225, 227
Citizens Opposed to Outrageous Politics 196

City Bank and Trust 166, 201
Civic Center 181, 200, 205, 214, 224-225
Civil Defense 78, 284
Claremore, OK 24
Clark, Jr., B.C. 94
Clark, Jim 200
Clinton, Bill 225-228, 242, 293
Cobb, Jerrie 277
Coles, Allen 167
Conference of Mayors 227
Cooper, Gordon 283
Cornett, Jack 167, 183, 186, 212
Cornett, Mick 259-260
Cory, Fran 8, 165, 222, 236
Couch, Jim 261
Crandall, Robert 184
Crawford, Dick 176
Crosstown Expressway 283, 285
Crystal Bridge 178, 292

D

Daily Oklahoman 175, 182-183, 193, 216
Darrell-Daniels, Shirley 201
Daugherty, Fred 69
Deck, Glenn 255, 294
Douglas Plant 29, 33
Dowell, A.L. 127, 132
Downtown Redevelopment Task Force 200
Draper, Sr., Stanley 91, 118, 253

E

Earlywine Park 287
Edmondson, J. Howard 76, 103, 278, 282-283
Edwards, Jay 181
Edwards, Mickey 181-182
Elgin, Mark 201
Elm Creek Reservoir 89-90
Evans, Roy 22

F

FAA 88, 282
Factory Distributing 281
Fairgrounds 205, 232, 245
Fallin, Mary 8, 228
Fallout Shelter 285
FBI 223, 225, 232-233
FEMA 225, 235
Fenstermacher, Richard L. 221
Ferguson, U.C. 59, 151
Fine, Dan 181, 186
Foshee, Jerry 253-254
Frankfurt, Short, Bruza 204-205, 207, 212-214, 217-218
Frosaker, Emily 262
FSB 8

G

Gaylord, Edward L. 217
Gaylord Family 158
General Motors 153
GEX 281

Gibson, Mildred 146
Gingrich, Newt 230-231
Godfrey, Arthur 71
Goldwater, Barry 103
Gonzales, Sam 232, 235
Gore, Al 242
Great Wall of China 268
Gridiron Club 133

H

Haikou, People's Republic of China 240, 267-268, 270
Haileyville, OK 19
Hall, Fred 201, 261
Hammons, John Q. 257
Hansen, Jon 179, 225
Hansen, Leroy 285
Harlow, Bryce 270
Harlow, Jr., James 200
Harris, Curtis P. 132
Harrison, Walter 42, 49, 52, 55-56, 62-63, 88
Hartshorne Sun 20
Hawthorne Elementary 152-153
Hearn, Paula 293
Heffron, Howard 41-42
Hefner, Robert 66, 259
Highlander Lanes 145
Hill, Archibald 128
Hillcrest Golf & Country Club 60, 151
Hite, Howard 167, 171

Hodges, Beverly 173,
186, 201
Hogan, Dan 181
HOK 204
Holman, Carleen 6-7
Horrow, Rick 8, 204-
205, 207, 212, 253
Horton, Chris 40
Horton, Clark 40
Humphries, Kirk 219,
257, 260, 294
Hupfeld, Stanley 181

I

Ingle, Clyde 181, 201
Inhofe, Jim 244
International Pressman's
Union 157
Istook, Ernest 222, 244

J

Jackson, W.K. 127-128
James, Goree 186, 201
Jarman, John 45, 57
Jaycee Janes 38, 60
Jaycees 39, 41-42, 151,
264
Jet 278
Jim Norick Arena 245
Johnson, Harold 283
Johnson, Willa 212
Johnstone, Bill 166-
167, 181, 201-202
Junior Hospitality Club
60

K

Kauffman, Chris 152-
153, 267
Keating, Cathy 232
Keating, Frank 8-9, 15,

223-224, 229, 231,
242
Keith, Craig 8
Keller, Nelson 124
Kennedy, John F. 103
Kerr, Robert S. 54, 83,
89, 284, 286
Kessler, William 90
Kimberling, Tag 94, 97
King, Jack 26, 145
King, Jr., Martin Luther
127, 287
King, Tom 201
Kirkpatrick, John 181
Krank, Mabel 77, 117
Koumaris, Alex 262
Koumaris, Angie 262

L

Lake Stanley Draper
91, 260
Latting, Patience 107,
116, 127, 141, 222
Library 200, 205, 207,
259-260, 262, 294-
295
Liebmann, Guy 253,
256
Light Rail 205
Lincoln Park Golf
Course 151
Lincoln Park Zoo 277
Long, Bob 270
Loria, Jeffrey 199
Lucas, Frank 230-231,
244
Luper, Clara 121-122,
124, 126-127, 132
Lybarger, Stan 181
Lyles, Jimmy 184, 202

M

Majors, Laure Vaught 8

MAPS 16-17, 176,
193, 199, 202, 204,
206-207, 209-213,
215-219, 228, 233,
239-241, 243-245,
247, 249, 253,255-
257, 259, 261, 271,
293
MAPS for Kids 193
Mars, Gary 8, 179,
223, 225, 232, 235
Martin, Dusty 181
Martin, Ed 184
Martin, Roy 281
Mathews, Mac 151
Mayor's Christmas
Party 75, 181, 281,
285, 293
Mayor's Conference for
Women 187, 292
Mayor's Disaster Relief
Fund 242
Mayor's Magazine 236
Mayor's Prayer Breakfast
221
McAuliffe, Mike 182,
271
McCaleb, Neal 292
McCarty, J.D. 103
McCollum, Merle 196
McConnell, J.R. 154
McGee Creek 175,
177, 260, 288
McGee, Dean 118
McLaughlin, Kelly 262
McPherson, Frank 202
Medallion Hotel 242
Meek, Wilson 146
Meridian Golf Course
152
Mid-Southwest Food
Service Convention
224

Miller, Earl 41-43,
45-46
Miller, Ed 181
Monroney, Mike 283,
287
Montgomery, John
226, 228
Moon, F.C. 77
Moon, F.D. 283
Moore, Rick 181-182,
202, 207, 212, 215,
226, 228, 237, 240,
253, 267-268
Moore, Vickie 9
Mummers Theatre 60,
109, 113
Murrah Federal
Building 220, 222-
223, 227-228, 230-
231, 235, 255, 293
Murray, Johnstone
53-54
Muskogee Phoenix 20
Muskogee Times 20
Myriad 175, 181, 196,
199, 203, 205, 209,
221, 224, 242, 246,
260, 289, 292, 294

N

NAACP 77, 207
NASCAR 272-273
National League of
Cities 138-139, 291
Neese, Terry 187, 292
Neighborhood Alliance
187
NHL 245, 250, 252,
293
Nickles, Don 230-231,
244
Nigh, George 9, 11,

16, 116, 266, 292
Nixon, Richard 289
Norick, Allison 240,
262
Norick Art Center 270
Norick, Benjamin 19
Norick Brothers
Printing 20-21, 24,
27, 38-39, 41, 53,
74,76, 145-146, 148-
149, 152-154, 156-
159, 163-164, 202,
266, 290
Norick, Carolyn 179,
212
Norick, Dorothy 21,
24, 29
Norick, Frances 21,
24, 169
Norick, George "Lon"
19-20, 22, 58
Norick, Henry 19-22,
39, 58, 63, 66, 70,
76, 153-154, 165
Norick, James 20-21,
23-28, 30-40, 43-46,
49-50, 52-60, 62-63,
65-66, 69-71, 74-78,
81, 83, 85-88, 90-91,
93-94, 96-99, 101-
104, 106-113, 115,
118-119, 121, 127,
129, 132, 135-136,
141, 151, 153-154,
161-163, 165, 167,
169, 171, 173, 175,
239-241, 253, 259-
262, 264-267, 270,
272
Norick, Kandy 262,
269
Norick, Lance 272-273

Norick, Madalynne 13,
24, 26-29, 32-35,
39-40, 45-46, 60-61,
63, 65-66, 70, 98-99,
192, 104, 107, 110,
135-139, 141, 148,
165, 262, 265, 267
Norick, Marjorie 21,
24, 169
Norick, Ron 26-29,
32-35, 37, 46, 50,
63, 65-66, 69,
110, 141, 143-149,
151-154, 156-159,
161-171, 173-175,
177-179, 181-183,
186-187, 189-191,
193-194, 196-204,
206-207, 209-212,
215, 217-2237,
239-245, 250-257,
259-262, 264-265,
267-273
Norick, Ruth 20-21,
25,70, 110, 153,
169, 240, 286
Norick, Vickie 39, 46,
66, 104, 147, 262,
265
Norman Naval Base
27, 30
Norman, OK 28
North Canadian River
200, 205, 271-272
Northwest Classen
High 143, 152
Nunn, Paul 283

O

OGE 200
Oklahoma City Airport
Trust 196, 198

Oklahoma City Blazers
159, 242, 293
Oklahoma City Cavalry
292
Oklahoma City
Chamber 184, 194,
201-202, 206-207,
237
Oklahoma City 89ers
211, 241
Oklahoma City Fire
Department 178,
224
Oklahoma City
Memorial 252
Oklahoma City Police
Department 55
Oklahoma City Stars
159
Oklahoma City
University 60, 93,
96, 101, 146, 148,
162-164, 265, 270-
271, 292
Oklahoma Gazette 239
Oklahoma Military
Academy 24, 27, 72
Oklahoma Publishing
Company 53, 158
"Oklahoma Standard"
16, 224, 229, 233,
236
Oldland, Robert 121-
127, 129, 132, 287
Olsmith, Kaye 6-7
OMCA 88
Orza, Vince 217

P

Pannetta, Leon 225,
227-228

Penn Square Mall 176,
291
Phillips, Glenda 39-40,
141, 167, 241
Planetarium 280
Pope Paul VI 267
Purser, I.G. 186, 201

Q

Quiroga, Mario 8

R

Rainbow, Jack 40
Ramsey, Lyle 280
Randal, Judy 179
Randal, Roger 179
Reagan, Ronald 175
Red Cross 61, 102,
280
Remington Park 179,
243
Reynolds, Allie 59
Reynolds and Reynolds
153, 158, 266
Richardson, Linda 187,
292
Roll, Jerry 154
Rowan & Martin 116,
288

S

St. Luke's Methodist
Church 270
San Antonio, TX 201
Sauter, Doug 243
SBC 223
Schwartz, Mark 173,
186, 212, 218, 226,
228, 233, 235,
252-254

Scott, Jim 167, 184,
186, 196-198
Shepherd (Mall) Plaza
278, 286, 289
Shirk, George 83, 91,
102, 105, 107, 112-
113, 115
Shrine Association 266
Sister Cities 270
Skirvin Hotel 52, 55,
62, 186, 243, 292
Spartan 281
Stewart, Ed 183-184
Stirling, Sheldon 87,
89
Strasbaugh, Paul 118
Switzer, Barry 291

T

Taft Jr. High 152
"Thank You, America"
Tour 237
Thompson, Jim 8
Tianamon Square 268
Times-Journal 20, 53
Tinstman, Robert 118-
119
Tolbert, III, James 201
Townsend, Ken 202
Tulakes Airport 279
Tulsa 176, 179, 184,
186-187
Turner, Roosevelt 288
Turner Turnpike 72
Twin Hills Golf &
Country Club 59,
106

U

United Airlines 187,
192-194, 196-199,
201, 205

University of Oklahoma 162, 204

Urban Renewal 76, 139, 202, 278, 280, 284-285, 287

U.S.S. *Chowanoc* 29, 32-33, 36

V

Vance, David 181

W

Waldron, Caroline 262

Waldron, Mike 262

Walters, David 194, 196, 293

Ware, William 102, 281, 284

Watts, J.C. 231

Waynoka, OK 22, 24

Welch, Jack 26

Wheat, Willis 162

White, Pete 167-168, 171, 201

Wiley Post Airport 279-280

Wilkes, Jack 93-94, 96-99, 101-102, 163, 286

Will Rogers World Airport 184

Williams, Chad 5

Williams, John 177

Willow Creek Golf & Country Club 151

Witt, James Lee 225

Wolf, Stephen 197

Y

YMCA 223, 252, 293

Young, Stanton 132